DON'T JUST STAND THERE!

a first book on Christian mission

MARTIN GOLDSMITH

InterVarsity Press
Downers Grove
Illinois 60515

© 1976 by Inter-Varsity Press, Leicester, England.
Published in America by InterVarsity Press, Downers Grove,
Illinois with permission from Universities and Colleges
Christian Fellowship, Leicester, England.

InterVarsity Press is the book-publishing division
of Inter-Varsity Christian Fellowship, a student movement
active on campus at hundreds of universities, colleges and
schools of nursing. For information about local and regional
activities, write IVCF, 233 Langdon St., Madison, WI 53703.

ISBN 0-87784-649-9
Library of Congress Catalog Card number: 76-49237

Printed in the United States of America

12	11	10	9	8	7	6	5	4	3	2
89	88	87	86	85	84	83	82	81		

Bookstore

Contents

2 25

29 Mar 85

70704

1 Optional extra?

'It's fantastic; it's like living in the days of the New Testament.' The students were thrilled. God had been working in a series of evangelistic talks in the Christian Union. Many students had accepted Christ as Saviour. Now came the task of helping these new believers to grow in their faith. An excited atmosphere of urgency ran through the group.

It was at this stage that I was due to lead a day's teach-in on missions. Only a relatively small number came.

'Sorry so few are here,' said the secretary, 'but people are so busy after these evangelistic meetings. They just don't have time for overseas mission.'

I wondered what the new Christians would be taught. How to pray and read their Bible; basic doctrines concerning sin, salvation and the Holy Spirit? Undoubtedly, but would they be taught anything at all about God's out-going love towards the whole world? They might be helped to witness among their own people in this country; would they be encouraged to have an active love for all men?

This highlights a basic weakness throughout our churches and Christian Unions. World-wide mission is an optional extra to be indulged in by those who are spiritually keen and who happen to be interested in it. Those who try to stimulate a belief that world mission is an integral part of the life of the church find that such exhortations fail to make much impact. Why?

Is it, perhaps, because we do not see world-wide mission as a basic theme of the whole of the Bible? So often missionary work is made to hinge on only a few verses: the Great Commission in Matthew 28; Acts 1:8; John 4:35;

Romans 10 : 14–17. As a speaker I attend large numbers of missionary meetings, and often wish that other passages could sometimes be used for the Bible Reading. Does mission really depend only on these few verses? If so, then it is surely right that mission should be a minor theme in the church's teaching. Ministers would be right not to mention overseas mission except when they happen to be expounding these particular verses – and if they are systematic in their exposition of the Bible, they would not come upon these passages very often.

But the whole Bible from Genesis to Revelation demonstrates God's love for all peoples and nations everywhere; He is the sovereign God over all the world. He has a purpose too for all nations. This purpose is quietly worked out through the centuries as described in the Bible. God made the world . . . God loved the world . . . God sent His Son into the world to redeem. And we look forward to the climax – 'a great multitude which no man could number, from every nation, from all tribes and peoples and tongues, standing before the throne and before the Lamb'.

Why do many ministers fail to teach world mission in their regular Bible exposition? Why do students fail to pass on this vision to new Christians? Why do many Christians of all ages and backgrounds consider overseas mission to be an optional extra? The fundamental reason is that they do not see it as a basic teaching of the whole of Scripture. It is a failure to grasp the biblical basis for mission that stops it being taught in the normal everyday programme of Bible teaching.

Christians love to dwell on the basic facts of their faith as we find them, for example, in Romans 1–8. They emphasize, too, that such doctrine must lead to practical Christian living as Paul teaches it in Romans 12–16. But what about the missing chapters Romans 9–11, where Paul teaches an out-going mission to Gentiles as well as to Jews? These key chapters are less well known. Romans teaches us, in fact, that *all* peoples are sinners, both Jews and Gentiles. All can be justified through faith in Christ and can know the sanctifying work of the Holy Spirit. Paul longs for the salvation of his own people – 'I could wish that I myself were accursed and cut off from Christ for the sake of my brethren, my kinsmen by race'. But he sees that their zeal for God was not enough to save them: they needed a 'righteousness that comes from God'. This God-given righteousness and salvation comes through faith and is therefore open to anyone of any nation. Gentiles too can be saved.

We today often forget that the early Christians were amazed to think that a Gentile might be saved – *we* marvel when we hear of a *Jew* becoming a Christian! In Romans 11 Paul shows God's New Testament strategy of mission, which is that the salvation of Gentiles will finally provoke Israel to jealousy and then Israel herself will return to the Lord.

The final section of this letter to the Romans begins with another well-known verse: 'I appeal to you therefore, brethren, by the mercies of God, to present your bodies as a living sacrifice' (Romans 12:1). What does this 'therefore' refer to? To the whole of Romans 1–11; to the whole of God's great plan of salvation for all nations, Jews and Gentiles. In this context we are to present our bodies. Paul is very practical and realistic – it is our bodies which are to be presented as a living sacrifice. God does not want any vague sacrifice of something merely spiritual – He wants our bodies. In the previous verses Paul shows that God's mercy to us is in order that others may receive mercy too. Now he appeals for sacrificial living on the basis of the mercies of God to all peoples – 'by the mercies of God present your bodies'. Dedicated, practical Christian living will include mission to all peoples.

So we see that the follow-up of those new student Christians lacked a full biblical perspective, if it did not involve missionary teaching. The Christian Union members were longing for the new Christians to grow into spiritual maturity and to be wholly committed to the Lord. Such dedication of our bodies to follow the Lord lacks a true biblical context if it is divorced from the concept of world mission.

2 Let your light shine

The initial atmosphere of bored cynicism gradually gave way to a growing interest. I was discussing modern missionary situations with a class of sixth formers. They began to see that Christians are not necessarily as out of date as they had imagined. Yet still the undercurrent of opposition could be felt.

One of the boys put up his hand. 'What right have you to thrust your religion down other people's throats?' he asked. The glint in his eye betrayed his thoughts. Such an original question would surely show the inadequacy of my Christian position. Little did he suspect that this criticism is frequently aimed at missionaries.

This question assumes various things which are actually not true. It assumes firstly that the missionary's task is to 'thrust' or force his Christian faith onto other people overseas. This is far from the truth. Further, it assumes that people overseas are so ignorant or gullible that they will swallow whole anything that we attempt to put down their throats. In fact it is often true that the more uneducated people are, the less ready are they to accept anything new – this is so in England. Equally if they are educated, they will not passively receive just anything offered to them! It happens also to be a general truth that what is forced down a throat is usually quickly coughed up again!

But this question makes one much more profound assumption of a more theological nature. It implies that there are different religions or even different gods for each people or area of the world. This is no new idea, as we learn from the story of Ahab and Benhadad.

In 1 Kings 20 King Ahab of Israel defeated the great Syrian King Benhadad. Benhadad's servants thought Israel had won the battle because it was fought on territory under Jehovah's authority – if the battle had been fought on the territory of the gods of Syria, then Benhadad would have won. 'The servants of the king of Syria said to him, "Their gods are gods of the hills, and so they were stronger than we; but let us fight against them in the plain, and surely we shall be stronger than they".'

The heathen have often thought of gods as geographically limited. Naaman had the same idea even after he had seen the greatness of the God of Israel. Elated at his miraculous healing, he realized that 'there is no god in all the earth but in Israel'. So, when he wanted to return to his native Syria, he asked the prophet, 'I pray you, let there be given to your servant two mules' burden of earth; for henceforth your servant will not offer burnt offering or sacrifice to any god but the Lord'. Naaman felt that the God of Israel could only be worshipped on Israelite soil, so he needed to take back to Syria a load of earth. He now knew that Jehovah was the only true God, but still he had in his mind the old heathen idea of a geographically-limited God.

In essence the beliefs of Naaman and of Benhadad's servants are the same as those of the more modern person who asks, 'Isn't their god as good as yours?' Theologians would reword this question by asking, 'Is God really universal?'

Genesis 1–11: God deals directly with all mankind
All of us have been tempted to sneak a glance at the last pages of an exciting detective novel. But most books are designed to be read systematically from the first page to the last. With the Bible, however, it seems to be the custom to concentrate on the last section with relatively little reference to the earlier parts. This is a pity, for the New Testament depends on the Old Testament for its background. It is virtually impossible to understand the meaning of the Gospels and Epistles (let alone the Book of Revelation) without some Old Testament background.

'The Word of God says . . .'; 'I believe in the Word of God, the Bible'. So say many earnest-minded and sincere young Christians; but have they actually *read* the Bible? Or have they read only a few small parts of it? It is the whole of the Bible that teaches the universal nature of God's control and God's love.

'Is God really universal?' – we asked that question just now and we need to start at Genesis 1 if we are to find the biblical answer. Genesis 1 is also where we begin to understand the demands of God for world mission.

God is universal

A Sunday School teacher stands up and begins to teach the story of creation. What a convenient story it is for a lesson to children! Visual aids are no problem. A circle with six segments is quickly stuck up on the flannelgraph. Pretty little drawings of sun, moon and stars find their place on one side; birds and other creatures on the other. And so the story of creation is taught. The children have learnt that God made the world. But have they seen the significance of this fact? Have they learnt how the Bible itself uses the creation story throughout the Old and New Testaments?

'The earth is the Lord's and the fulness thereof, the world and those who dwell therein; for he has founded it upon the seas and established it upon the rivers'. The Psalmist does not merely state that God made the world; he draws from this fact the conclusion that God is *Lord* both of the world and of all the people in it. He is the universal God.

King Hezekiah was in a desperate situation. The much-feared armies of Assyria had engulfed state after state. How could the puny land of Judah expect to stand against such an onslaught? There was only one answer. Hezekiah prayed before the Lord, 'O Lord the God of Israel, who art enthroned above the cherubim, thou art the God, thou alone, of all the kingdoms of the earth; thou hast made heaven and earth'. Taunting him the Assyrian Rabshakeh mocked any idea of trusting Israel's God to deliver Jerusalem from the Assyrians. 'Behold, you have heard what the kings of Assyria have done to all lands, destroying them utterly', the Rabshakeh threatened, 'and shall you be delivered? Have the gods of the nations delivered them, the nations which my fathers destroyed?' The Rabshakeh assumed that the God of Israel would have no power over the armies of the Assyrians.

But Hezekiah's faith stretched out to a universal God who had power over all peoples, not only over His own Israel. 'Thou art the God, thou alone, of all the kingdoms of the earth.' On what was this faith based? Did Hezekiah have good reason to believe that the God of Israel was more than a local national God? Yes! The God of Israel is the God who *created* heaven and earth; therefore He is the 'God of all the kingdoms of the earth'. All was made by God and all is therefore under God's power and control.

Hezekiah goes even further and deduces from all this that the gods of other nations are not gods at all – they are just 'the work of men's hands'. Man-made gods are powerless – whether they are made by men's hands or by men's minds. But the Creator God is the one who can save Jerusalem, Hezekiah, and us.

The Sunday School teacher – and everyone else who teaches about creation – should bring out the corollary that the God who creates also therefore owns and controls the whole of His creation. Since He is the universal God, He, and He alone, is to be worshipped by all people in all nations.

Worship the Creator, not the created

Hezekiah drew the obviously logical conclusion: if God is the one true Creator God, then the worship of other gods is wrong. This is a basic principle for mission. Jehovah ought to be the God of all peoples; He alone should be worshipped and served. Sadly He is unknown today to many all over the world and is therefore robbed of the glory He should be given. The honour due to God alone is often given to idols, spirits or man-made deities. So Paul says that people 'exchanged the truth about God for a lie and worshipped and served the creature rather than the Creator'.

This accusation by Paul is obviously true in those

religions which practise idolatry. In the West today it is not popular to criticize other religions, but the Christian can only be saddened when he sees people worshipping the Buddha or other created beings.

Tucked away in the back streets of Singapore stands an unusual Temple. Behind the huge golden figure of the Buddha there lies another idol – a sleeping Buddha. His body is covered with a beautiful cloth. Men and women come to pray and worship. Before they can do so, however, they must wake him up. They slap the stone statue three times. Surely now the Buddha is awake! Then they worship. This is typical of the more obviously idolatrous worship of many people all over the world.

However, it is not only in gross idolatry that men worship the created rather than the Creator. It is equally true of those more refined and sophisticated religions which have developed through human wisdom. They have their philosophical ideas of a divine power which may or may not be personal, but is this truly the Creator who reveals Himself in the Bible and supremely in the Person of His Son, Jesus Christ of Nazareth?

In the traditionally Christian western world many today are reacting against institutionalized religion with its emphasis on doctrinal and ethical conformity. Such religion often lacks spiritual vitality, spontaneity and open-hearted love. Truth, rather than life, is highlighted as the essential characteristic of true faith. The balance of Jesus as the way, the truth *and* the life has frequently been lost. Today, many swing the pendulum to the other extreme, looking for spiritual 'life' at the expense of a biblical 'truth' which is firmly rooted in historical fact. In the search for an experience which demonstrates spiritual life and power, Eastern religions with their mysticism and unstructured approach have great appeal. Christians should, of course, see the failures of the church of God and repent of our sin. We sympathize with those who turn disillusioned to eastern religions or to the occult. Nevertheless, our mission is to call all men everywhere to follow and worship the one Creator God through Jesus Christ.

Some religions, such as Islam and Judaism, do not worship the creation, for they have a heritage which stems from the Old Testament. They worship one God, but sadly they have missed the Way. To the Muslim, Muhammad is like a signpost pointing to the way; but Jesus said, 'I *am* the Way'. It is considered blasphemous to an orthodox Muslim to talk of knowing God or being united with Him. God is too great for such a personal relationship, they say. Even in heaven God is not to be found. Yet as a Christian one feels that a heaven without God's personal presence is more akin to hell.

The Creation story demonstrates that God alone is to be worshipped, not His creation. And the New Testament affirms that He is to be worshipped through Jesus Christ, the Way.

Some years ago it was common among theologians to try to define what are the basic elements of the apostles' evangelistic sermons in the Book of Acts. People were trying to find out what are the central facts of the gospel. Now it is realized that the apostles preached somewhat differently to their various audiences. Some basic elements are in all the sermons – *e.g.* the cross and the resurrection. But the fact of creation is not in all the sermons. It is only in those to the Gentiles. Gentiles worshipped mythical, man-made Greek and Roman gods; they also worshipped spirits. They did not know the Creator God, and so the apostles start their sermons to the Lycaonians and the Athenians with 'the God who made the world and everything in it'. When the Lycaonians wanted to worship Paul and Barnabas because they mistook them for Zeus and Hermes, Paul urged them to 'turn from these vain things to a living God who made the heaven and the earth and the sea and all that is in them'. With those who worship the created rather than the Creator, the evangelist needs to start with Genesis 1 and 2.

The Jews did not worship the created, so the apostles' sermons to Jews do not emphasize the creation story. Today too we often need to learn that our witness cannot be the same to all people – God varies His approach according to the needs of the individual. Each person and each race in each generation has its own background. Different aspects of biblical truth may need to be brought out with different people.

Even now in the twentieth century many people are still worshipping the created and the missionary message for such people will need to begin with creation.

My wife and I worked for some years with the Indonesian churches in north Sumatra, among the Karo Batak people. Behind our home rose two splendid volcanoes, both of which belched smoke at all times. A certain awesome wonder and beauty surrounded these ominous peaks. The local people were convinced that spirits inhabited them. One day we were invited to climb one of these volcanoes with a group of local Christian friends. Early in the morning we struggled through the dank jungle and then up across the steep stony slopes to the rim of the crater.

Beside the path lay sacrificial offerings to the spirits – eggs, bananas and other food, together with cigarettes whose smoke curled up from the forked sticks in which they were placed. The fear of the spirits is real.

Finally we reached the top and gazed down into the crater with its pool of sickly light blue water. Sulphurous yellow smoke spurted from cracks in the earth's surface. The noise was like that of a great steam engine; the smell like that of rotten eggs. But we had no time at that moment for either the sounds or the smells, for the local Christians were leading us in a symbolic action. They picked up stone after stone, hurling them down into the crater. 'Spirit-worshippers would not dare do this,' they shouted, 'they would fear the spirits of the volcano. Throwing stones would make the spirits angry.' And yet more stones bounced gaily from rock to rock as they were cast down into the crater. One fell into a crack from which smoke issued; it was hurled into the air by the irresistible power from within the volcano. 'We Christians are not scared of spirits, so we show it by throwing stones.' My wife and I joined in the action; more stones skipped down into the depths, knocking rock after rock as if daring the angry spirits of the volcano to prove themselves. 'We worship only the Creator; there is no need to worship anything else.'

The obvious beauty and power of nature move man to a deep sense of spiritual reality. The animist sees the uncontrollable power and awe-inspiring life of nature, in which he senses the lurking presence of spirits. Christians, too, see God in the loveliness around them. Christians have traditionally enjoyed meditation and prayer in the midst of beautiful scenery which heightens our awareness of God and His goodness. Man's whole being responds to the spiritual influence of nature. But his reaction to nature will vary according to his underlying beliefs. Those with a basic belief in God may find their faith and love for the Creator deepened. Those whose minds are inclined to a fear of spirits will find confirmation of the reality of spirit activity as they contemplate nature. Even Hitler was strengthened in his philosophy of life by his vision of nature; but he saw the cruelty, not the beauty of it. He was therefore moved to say, 'Why should not man be as cruel as nature?' But God's purpose is that 'ever since the creation of the world his invisible nature, namely his eternal power and deity, has been clearly perceived in the things that have been made'.

The Karo Christians taught us the meaning of the creation story for mission. Their evangelistic teaching and preaching were always based first on the fact of creation – and from this they drew the conclusion that man is to worship the Creator and not the spirits of created nature.

God's aim for the world and for man

'God saw everything that he had made, and behold, it was very good.' Yet this morning we read our newspapers and we saw the world God had made – 'and behold, it was not very good'! The contrast is so extreme that the Bible seems almost naïve.

In Genesis we see what is God's aim for the world and for man. He wants the cosmos to be 'very good' and He wants men of all races to be 'in the image of God', like God. It is therefore the missionary task to make both man and his environment more akin to God's original purpose.

But from Genesis 3 onwards we see the growing damage done by sin. As Karl Marx rightly said, 'original sin is

17

everywhere at work'. In Genesis 3–11 the world develops on twin tracks – one of growing sin and another of God's answer in salvation.

The tragedy of man's Fall in Genesis 3 is immediately followed by God's starting of the line of descent which should lead to the coming of the Saviour. Because of God's promise to her, Eve thought the Saviour would come immediately. Cain was born and she exclaimed, 'I have gotten a man, the Lord' (my translation). She thought her baby was already the promised Lord, the coming Messiah. But Cain was no paragon of messianic virtue – he was a fallen human being with original sin in evidence. No wonder Eve seems to have been somewhat disappointed – she called her second son 'Abel', 'Vanity'. Many a modern mother might sympathize!

In the days of Noah sin came to a climax – and so did God's work of salvation. Sin ruled on the earth. God's judgment swept through mankind. But God's salvation was granted to those few who had faith in Him. Yet God's grace to Noah was not the end of the story. Noah and his family came out of the ark, planted a vineyard, drank of the wine – 'and became drunk'.

So the history of sin continued. In Genesis 11 man's sinful pride came again to such an extreme that God had to step in with further judgment. The building of the Tower of Babel was judged by the scattering of men into all parts of the earth with a confusion of languages.

Until this time God dealt directly with all mankind, but now He deals specifically with one race. This was not because of partiality, but in order that through them His salvation might be brought to all men. In Genesis 12 God develops a new stage in His strategy.

Abraham – God's outreach through a minority

Karl Marx believed that history would so develop that the whole mass of the proletariat would rise spontaneously as a group in revolution. Lenin was more practical; he said that it was necessary to have a small well-trained élite to lead the masses into revolution.

In Genesis 1–11 God deals with the whole mass of mankind as a group. But the development of sin had made a new approach necessary if He were to bring His salvation to all peoples. God therefore called Abraham and his children to be His instruments to demonstrate God's glory to all mankind. Jesus later used the same method – He chose a small group of disciples through whom He was to influence the whole world.

Israel has often forgotten the purpose of God's choice of her as His people. Even today many Jews still ignore God's aims for mankind and feel that the God of Israel is for Jews only. However, more spiritually-minded Jews like Martin Buber see Israel as God's instrument of blessing for the nations. 'Jerusalem is the gateway of the nations. It is up to us to seek its salvation, which is the salvation of the nations', Buber affirms. Through the Jew God will bring salvation to all nations. This was the purpose of God's call of Abraham. 'I will bless you . . . so that you will be a blessing.' 'By you all the families of the earth will be blessed.' Through Abraham and his children God's blessing was to pass to all nations, to all the families of the earth.

Here was a new stage in God's strategy for the world. His glory would be clearly seen in one family. The blessings of God would be so obviously upon Abraham that all men would see the reality of his God. Jesus repeated this idea when He said, 'Let your light so shine before men, that they may see your good works, and give glory to your Father who is in heaven'. This was not, however, an out-going missionary call, but a challenge to live a life which reflected God's glory and blessing to such an extent that men were drawn spontaneously to faith in the Lord. The later New Testament emphasis on outgoing mission is based on the Old Testament concept of the glory of God being seen in the lives of God's people.

The theory is good; the practice is often sadly disappointing. 'We have Christians resident in every student hostel,' a student leader told me. The secretary of a church pointed out on a map all the different streets and areas where the church members lived. My heart thrilled to think of the potential of God's people placed so strategically. Surely the world will see God's glory in the lives of these Christians in their street or in their hostel! This must be the setting for a turning to the Lord – people should see our good works and so come to glorify our Father in heaven. But does it work out? So often the glory of the Lord is not reflected adequately in our lives.

So it was with Abraham. Immediately after his call his large flocks faced starvation. Famine was stalking through the land. Egypt still had corn and Abraham took his wife in search of food. This was no missionary journey, but God was sending His servant to live temporarily in Egypt for economic reasons. We can imagine the angels dancing with delight! What an opportunity! God's man was to be resident in Egypt. Yes! Egypt! Surely Pharaoh and his people would now see that the God of Israel is the universal God. What joy to think of the people of Egypt turning in repentance and faith to the Lord through the witness of Abraham's life!

But how, in fact, did it work out? Sarah was very pretty. Egyptian men had a reputation as regards girls. Abraham was afraid. Perhaps the Egyptians would kill him so that they could freely take Sarah. He was not worried for Sarah's honour – his one fear was that he himself might be killed.

'Say that you are my sister,' he told her, 'that it may go well with me because of you.' And so they entered the land of Egypt. All eyes were turned on Sarah – she was beautiful. The princes of Egypt told Pharaoh of her beauty and soon Pharaoh took her from Abraham: 'the woman was taken into Pharaoh's house'. We can imagine Sarah's agony. But Abraham was happy – Pharaoh gave him sheep, oxen and all sorts of wealth.

How could Pharaoh see the glory of God in Abraham's life? He could not possibly do so.

Then God stepped in. The Lord sent plagues on Pharaoh and all his household. Pharaoh had to ask why he was so afflicted with these plagues. The secret came out. Sarah was Abraham's wife. God's moral laws were being broken and judgment was the result. God's glory could now be seen through His judgment, but not through the life of His servant.

And so it was through most of Israel's history. God's longing was frustrated – the nations did not see His glory in the life of Israel as a people.

But the vision remained. Israel still dreamt of the nations pouring into Zion to offer their worship to the God of Israel. They dreamt of all the families of the earth coming with their gifts and offerings to the Temple.

Occasionally this vision was actually fulfilled. The days of David and Solomon form a high-water mark in the history of Israel. Solomon's ships came every three years, bringing their cargoes of gold and silver, ivory, apes and peacocks. Chariots and horses of prime quality were imported from Egypt. Silver became as common in Jerusalem as stone; cedar as plentiful as any common tree. All peoples were amazed at the riches of Israel – a sure sign that the God of Israel was pouring out His blessing on them.

It was not only Israel's wealth that drew the nations in admiration. 'Men came from all peoples to hear the wisdom of Solomon, and from all the kings of the earth, who had heard of his wisdom.' God gave Solomon unrivalled wisdom and 'largeness of mind'; he 'uttered three thousand proverbs and his songs were a thousand and five'. Solomon's fame 'was in all the nations round about'.

Hiram, King of Tyre, was drawn to Israel's God through Solomon. The Queen of Sheba heard reports of Solomon's unusual wisdom. Such exaggerated stories were common enough in the flowery language of those parts, but the stories of Solomon's greatness were unbelievable. She doubted them. Finally she could not resist – she would find out for herself whether they were true. She set off for Jerusalem with a great caravan of camels, loaded with gifts of spices, gold and jewels.

What a palace! Look at Solomon's servants! Why, they wear clothing fit for a king! And then she saw the long lines of animals being led towards the Temple. 'Why are so many animals being taken to the Temple?' she asked. She learnt of the system of sacrifices which Jehovah had ordained. 'What a God He must be to be worth such numbers of sacrifices!' Then she heard Solomon's words of wisdom – he decided his people's quarrels; he uttered his proverbs and his songs. The Queen of Sheba was overwhelmed and 'there was no more spirit in her'. Humbled and convinced, she admitted, 'the report was true which I heard in my own land of your affairs and of your wisdom'. Through her appreciation of Solomon's wisdom, she came to the stage where she could say, 'Blessed be the Lord your God'.

Solomon never went to Tyre to preach to Hiram; he did not visit Sheba to evangelize the Queen. They saw the splendour of God's blessing in the wisdom and life of Solomon; so they came spontaneously to Zion to see that the God of Israel is God indeed.

In Genesis 1–11 God dealt directly with all men in His offer of salvation, in His desire to restore the image of God in man. In the remainder of the Old Testament God reached out in blessing to all the families of the earth through a specially called minority, through Abraham and the people of Israel. The nations were to see in the life of His followers the reality of the one true God and be drawn spontaneously to Him. Both before and after the call of Abraham, God's desire was that all men of all nations should come to worship Him and so return increasingly to being 'like God', 'very good'.

But what about God's missionary outreach in the New Testament?

3 The Light of the world

Jesus fulfils the Old Testament

Jesus is the perfect Jew. He fulfils the calling of God to
Israel. In the days of David and Solomon the heathen had
seen something of the glory of God, but never in perfect
purity. By contrast, in Jesus of Nazareth could be seen the
very image of God, full of grace and truth. It is symbolic
therefore that certain Gentiles came spontaneously to Him.
The Wise Men came from the East. They were not evangelized by an out-going missionary activity – they came to
Jesus. John 12 tells us that some Greeks came to Jesus. No-
one went to evangelize them – they came of their own
accord to see Him. The Roman centurion also saw the
event of the cross and 'praised God'.

Perhaps the clearest example of a Gentile who came
spontaneously to Jesus is the Canaanite woman in Matthew
15. Her daughter was demon-possessed and there seemed no
escape from the turmoil this situation caused in her life.
Then she heard of Jesus, the man who works miracles of
healing, the man who teaches with authority and lives in
purity. Perhaps Jesus could help? She heard that He was
coming to her district. The crowds gathered, but she was
not to be put off by all the onlookers. She went out to meet
Him and cried out, 'Have mercy on me, O Lord, Son of
David.' What would Jesus say or do now?

She waited expectantly for an answer, but Jesus paid no
attention. She persevered, crying out again and again.
Still no answer. Jesus' disciples began to get annoyed
with her. She was making a real nuisance of herself
and it was embarrassing in front of so many people.

Besides, she was only a Gentile woman. 'Send her away,' they begged Jesus. Some of the crowd might have remembered Jesus' reaction when the disciples had tried to send some children away from Him. 'Suffer the little children to come unto Me,' He had said. Would He now rebuke His disciples again and invite this Gentile woman to come to Him with her requests? No! Jesus seemed to agree with the disciples: 'I was sent only to the lost sheep of the house of Israel,' He said.

The Canaanite woman had called Jesus 'Son of David'; she knew He was called to and for the Jews. But would He extend His healing ministry to Gentiles? She persevered yet again. Kneeling before Him, she begged, 'Lord, help me'. Bewilderingly, Jesus continued to rebuff her pleadings. 'It is not fair to take the children's bread and throw it to the dogs.' Jesus, the fulfilment of the Old Testament calling of Israel, was to feed the Jews, not the Gentiles. He never went purposely to Gentiles. They came to Him – and this woman was not to be put off; she was determined to come to Him and find salvation for her daughter. 'Even the dogs eat the crumbs that fall from their master's table,' came her meek answer. Jesus saw her determined faith, and the girl was healed.

God had said to Abraham, 'By you all the families of the earth will be blessed.' In Jesus the Gentiles saw the wonder of the unique God and came to Him to find that blessing. When this Old Testament vision was fulfilled, then the way was open for God to develop to the next stage His world strategy for the nations. The spontaneous in-coming of the Gentiles had to precede any out-going evangelistic mission to all the world.

Jesus and the Samaritans

We have seen that Jesus Himself went primarily to the Jews, although Gentiles came spontaneously to Him. His vision for the future, however, was the out-going mission of His church to all nations. God's method was to change from the passive testimony of Israel's life to the active evangelistic mission of the church to all nations. God had never abandoned His desire for the salvation of all peoples. This had been seen clearly in Genesis 1–11. It continued through the rest of Old Testament times, when God drew Gentiles to Himself through the life-witness of Israel. Now Jesus' disciples were to be sent out to all the world in active mission.

But there was a fearful prejudice to overcome. Jews despised Gentiles. The common names given by Jews to Gentiles were 'dogs', 'sinners'. Contact with a Gentile made a Jew ritually unclean. The only hope for a Gentile in Jewish eyes was to become like a Jew and follow the Jewish Law. Jesus knew therefore that it was unduly hard to ask His disciples to go to Gentiles – the way to this had to be prepared more gradually. So He encouraged them to work with Samaritans as a half-way house between Jews and Gentiles.

This reflects the nature of God. He does not demand from His people more than they can give at their present stage. Men often fail to be equally gentle and patient. A young Christian is too often expected to achieve the moral and spiritual standards of someone who has been for many years in the faith. God develops His children stage by stage, step by step.

So Jesus prepared the way for mission to the Samaritans. Even this was not easy. In the years before Jesus was born, political leaders had done much to improve Jew-Samaritan relations, but this improvement had not lasted.

In AD 7 some Samaritan trouble-makers came down to Jerusalem and insolently scattered the bones of dead animals in the Temple. The Jews were furious that their Temple had been desecrated. Relations between the two neighbouring peoples grew bitter. This was in AD 7, and Jesus must have been aged about eleven or twelve at that time. At the age of twelve Jesus was taken up to the Temple for the Passover. Every Jewish boy looked forward eagerly to his first Passover at the Temple. The religious atmosphere was tense with anticipation – and the resentment against the blaspheming intruders from Samaria burned bitterly in the hearts of all pious Jews. So Jesus grew up through the impressionable teenage years in this atmosphere of racial tension. 'Jews have no dealings with Samaritans,' the woman of Samaria said to Jesus as they talked by the well. Jesus must have smiled at such an understatement.

One day Jesus decided to go up to Jerusalem. Instead of taking a route by which He would avoid the contamination of walking through Samaritan territory, He purposely went by the direct way. He sent messengers ahead to prepare food and lodging *en route*. The Samaritan villagers asked where Jesus wanted to go. To Jerusalem? In that case, they did not want Him in their villages. They would not receive Him. Why should Samaritans receive Jewish travellers on their way to Jerusalem? James and John, the Sons of Thunder, saw their chance. They hated Samaritans. Perhaps Jesus would punish them for not receiving Him. 'Lord, do you want us to bid fire come down from heaven and consume them?' they demanded. One can imagine them almost rubbing their hands in gleeful anticipation of this judgment on their enemies.

But Jesus rebuked them: 'You do not know what manner of spirit you are of.' Racial and religious bitterness can so easily invade and spoil a disciple's life. The Sons of Thunder were keener to call down fire on their Samaritan enemies than to bring to them the salvation of the God of Israel. But Jesus added, 'The Son of Man came not to destroy men's lives but to save them.' And so He began to teach His followers that the saving mission of Christ is not only to Israel, but also to the wider circle of the Samaritans.

In the very next chapter of Luke's Gospel Jesus tells the story of the Good Samaritan. This parable is often said to teach merely that one should help people in need. And of course it is true that love for one's neighbour must include practical help. But even the Jewish writings of this period are full of moral instruction on how men should do good to others. The Rabbis required no support from Jesus in telling people that they should be charitable to the poor and kind to the needy. If this parable has no greater significance than that, then it is desperately commonplace.

It was a *Samaritan* who helped the Jew in this revolutionary parable. The Samaritan therefore proved to be neighbour to the Jew by the roadside. His was a love which broke through the norms of racial and religious barriers, overcoming prejudice and hatred. Jesus told the lawyer, 'Go and do likewise.'

So the parable stresses that love for one's neighbour means reaching out through the prejudices of race – or indeed through any barriers. It reaches to those racial groups or those segments of population which are disliked or shunned by others. In this way the disciples were learning that God's salvation and love goes out to Samaritans as well as to Jews. The basic ministry of Jesus Himself was to the lost sheep of the house of Israel, but He was preparing the way for His disciples to have a wider ministry after His death and resurrection. 'Greater things than these shall you do,' He said. The work of the incarnate Jesus was relatively limited, but He opened the door for the greater task of the disciples.

The disciples would be much criticized if they were to extend the offer of salvation to Samaritans also. Jesus helped in this by setting an example. Outside the Samaritan town of Sychar stood a well. Here Jesus talked alone to a Samaritan woman of evil repute. A Jew talking to a Samaritan! A bachelor in his early thirties talking alone to a woman! And a woman with a low reputation too!

One can imagine how the tongues wagged. But this bold love for His neighbour, breaking through current ideas of propriety, led to the woman's believing and then sharing her faith with others in her town. The tongues did wag – but about Jesus as the Messiah!

The disciples watched and learnt from their Master. He was taking them gently towards mission even to Gentiles, to those who were considered to be beyond the limits of the kingdom. God had always longed for His salvation to reach to the uttermost parts of the earth, so that peoples who were 'no people' should become God's own possession.

Jesus and the Gentiles

We have seen already that Jesus did not have an out-going ministry to Gentiles during His life on earth. A few Gentiles came spontaneously to Him, but He did not go out to them.

There is one possible exception to this: we find it in Matthew 15.

In verses 10–20 Jesus prepared the way for work among Gentiles by preaching against the external legalism which prevailed at that time. Spiritual cleanness, He asserted, does not depend on externals. Man is not separated from God by the foods he eats, or by the failure to observe petty rules on hand-washing. It is what comes out of the heart which defiles a man. Reflecting later on this teaching, Mark adds 'thus he declared all foods clean'. Sin is a disease of a man's heart. This section of Matthew's Gospel is closely related to Acts 10 where Peter also is called to extend his preaching to the Gentiles. That chapter starts with the same preparatory teaching concerning external legalism. Peter was given a frightful vision of a sheet full of ritually unclean animals. Then he was told to kill and eat. His stomach must have turned at the thought. 'No, Lord,' he expostulated, 'for I have never eaten anything that is common or unclean.' But the voice came to him again: 'What God has cleansed, you must not call common.'

Evidently Peter had been prepared to some extent for this devastating revelation, for his attitude to traditional laws was already weakened. He was staying in the house of a tanner, and this in itself shows that Peter had already abandoned 'Rabbinic scrupulosities'. The hides of dead animals made a tanner's yard ritually unclean. Rabbinic law said that such a yard must be at least fifty cubits away from any town. Rabbi Akiba comments that it should be still further if located to the west of a town because of the prevailing winds!

It was imperative that God should break down Peter's scruples concerning the externals of the Law before He could call him to the wider ministry to the Gentiles. So also in Matthew 15, Jesus taught against externalism in religion before going on in Matthew 15 : 21–28 to the encounter with the single Gentile Canaanite woman. In Acts 10, too, the vision led on to Peter's meeting with a single Gentile, Cornelius.

Both in Acts 10 and in Matthew 15 the Gentile came

spontaneously to Jesus and to Peter without any out-going evangelistic activity. But afterwards, in Matthew 15:29, Jesus purposely moved on into the Gentile area of the Decapolis and so made Himself available to the larger crowds of Gentiles. It could be said that this was an exception to the rule that Jesus never went out to the Gentiles, but on the other hand in 15:30 we read that 'great crowds *came to Him*'. He took the initiative in entering their territory and they flocked of their own accord to Him. As they came, He healed – with the result that 'they glorified the God of Israel'. The universal God was still thought of primarily as the national God of Israel.

In Matthew 15:32 and the verses following, Jesus led the disciples into the feeding of these non-Jewish crowds. When Jesus had fed the Jewish crowd of 5,000 it had been the disciples who had taken the lead in suggesting that something be done for them. Now with a Gentile crowd it has to be Jesus who calls His disciples to Him and says, 'I am unwilling to send them away hungry . . . I have compassion on the crowd.' So Jesus began to show that the God of Israel is willing to show love to all nations. In this way He was preparing His followers for the wider outreach of the future.

It was commonly accepted in Jewish thought that one sign of the coming of the Messiah was that His kingdom would be universal; all peoples would come in to Zion. When Jesus fed the Gentile crowd, therefore, the Pharisees and Sadducees wanted to know what right He had to do so. It is unfortunate that our Bibles divide 16:1–4 from the previous verses by a chapter division.

What happened next was that the Jews asked for a sign to prove that He had the right to widen His ministry to Gentile circles. But Jesus refused: 'An evil and adulterous generation seeks for a sign, but no sign shall be given to it except the sign of Jonah.' They should not have needed another sign; they had already been given a clear sign in that Jesus had gone to the Gentiles. That was the sign of Jonah, for Jonah was the sole example in the Old Testament of an out-going evangelistic ministry to Gentiles.

The way is now open for the preaching of the gospel to

men of all nations. Jesus has fulfilled the Old Testament in His perfect life, reflecting the glory of God and drawing Gentiles in to the God of Israel. He has also opened the door for outreach to Samaritans and even to Gentiles. The next chapter in God's strategy for the nations can now begin.

4 Your God reigns

Jesus and John the Baptist came preaching the kingdom of God. It was a familiar concept to their hearers. If, then, we are to understand God's purpose in mission, we must first examine what the Bible means by this concept of God's kingdom.

The early chapters of Genesis showed God's sovereign reign over all His creation. All men were to be subject to the Creator; the whole world was to be His kingdom.

When the world rebelled against God's rule, He chose to exercise His kingship over the people of Israel. But He never abandoned the over-all purpose that all peoples should own Him as King. Accordingly He gave the prophets the vision that kings and peoples from all over the world would come in to Zion to do homage to the King of Kings. Men of all nations would come in pilgrimage to pay tribute to the God of Israel; and the people of Israel would share in His reign, for the nations would also serve them. The rule of God in His kingdom was to be evidenced by the submission of the nations to His elect (see Ps. 60; Ps. 72 : 8–11; Is. 42 : 1–6; 56 : 6; 60 : 1–7, 12–16).

Israel was established as a theocracy with God as her head. The leaders of Israel were always to be subject to Him. The Law of the Lord was the basis of national life. Nothing was secular – all of life was to be lived in obedience to the heavenly King. This ideal was constantly challenged by the sinful disobedience of God's people and was finally shattered by their determination to have a human king like all the nations round about them.

Israel's desire to have a human king over them came as

no surprise to God, of course. Before the Jews came to Canaan He had already told Moses in Deuteronomy 17 : 14, 'When you come to the land which the Lord your God gives you, and you possess it and dwell in it, and then say, "I will set a king over me, like all the nations that are round about me"; you may indeed set as king over you him whom the Lord your God will choose.' And the king was commanded in the following verses to be subject to the Lord in humble and moral obedience to the Law.

Nevertheless, God made it clear to Samuel in 1 Samuel 8 : 7 that 'they have not rejected you, but they have rejected me from being king over them'; and then God proceeded to inform Samuel of the oppressive rule that the kings of Israel would exercise over His people. And so we are told later that Saul 'took the kingship'; the kingdom of God was usurped by mere man and Israel was to pay the consequences. Man always suffers when God's kingship is not recognized.

Although Israel chose to put a man in the place of God as king over them, it remained true that the sovereignty of God was not impaired. It was God who chose Saul – and likewise the kings who came after him. When David failed to live up to the standards God had set for the kings of Israel, it was said to David, 'The Lord has given the kingdom into the hand of your son Absalom'; the rise and fall of kings is always under God's sovereign control. But that did not prevent Israel from suffering God's inevitable judgment for their rebellious rejection of Jehovah as King.

The Jews always looked forward, therefore, to the day when God would again establish His kingdom in Israel and rule over them Himself. The prophets longed for the coming of the messianic kingdom; Isaiah sang of it: 'The government will be upon his shoulder. . . . Of the increase of his government and of peace there will be no end, upon the throne of David, and over his kingdom to establish it, and to uphold it with justice and with righteousness from this time forth and for evermore' (Is. 9 : 6, 7). The Rabbis emphasized the coming kingdom of heaven and called it 'the Truth of the Torah'. Rabbinic teaching on the coming kingdom is also beautifully expressed in the prayers of the synagogue. For example in the New Year Kingship Benediction Jews pray: 'Our God and God of our Fathers reign Thou in Thy glory over the whole universe, and be exalted above all the earth in Thine honour, and shine forth in the splendour and excellence of Thy might, upon all the inhabitants of Thy world, that whatsoever hath been created may understand that Thou hast made it, and whatsoever hath breath in its nostrils may say, "The Lord God of Israel is King and His dominion ruleth over all".'

Martin Buber, the great Jewish thinker of our own century, also saw that 'the realization of the all-embracing rulership of God is the Proton and Eschaton of Israel'. He likewise quotes with favour another theologian's comment that the very meaning of the word 'Israel' is 'May God manifest Himself as Lord, Ruler!'

We are not surprised, therefore, that John the Baptist came with the message that the kingdom of heaven was at hand. Jesus too came with the same message: 'The time is fulfilled, and the kingdom of God is at hand.' What did the Jews picture when they heard those words? Their minds went back to the prophetic descriptions of the coming kingdom.

Four basic characteristics are to be found in the Old Testament descriptions of God's kingdom – the kingdom that should have been experienced in Israel, but actually came into being through the coming of the Messiah and will finally be perfected at His coming in glory.

1 God's kingdom is universal

Luke 13 : 29 clearly states that 'men will come from east and west, and from north and south, and sit at table in the kingdom of God', reminding us of Jesus' feeding of the Gentile crowd in Matthew 15. Likewise in the parable in which Jesus likens the kingdom of God to a grain of mustard seed, He says that the birds of the air will make nests in its shade – a picture of the nations of the world finding rest in God's kingdom.

The Rabbis stressed the universal significance of the so-called *Shema*, the key verse of Deuteronomy 6 : 4, 'Hear, O Israel: the Lord our God is one Lord.' The unity of God implies that there can be no other gods and so the Talmud in Berachoth 13 says that the *Shema* declared God as King in the four corners of the world. He is God over all the earth and over all the peoples of the world.

But we have already said a good deal about the universality of the kingdom of God. We must now move on to the other three characteristics of righteousness, justice and peace. The prophecy in Is. 9 : 7, already quoted, makes clear that the messianic King's rule will be characterized by everlasting peace, justice and righteousness. We find the same idea in Isaiah 60 where the prophet looks forward to the day when Israel's overseers will be peace and her taskmasters righteousness (Is. 60 : 17); and in verse 14 those who oppressed and despised Israel would be brought low before her and so justice would be established.

2 Righteousness

The Jews believed that God's kingdom and His glorious presence in Israel could be established only when Israel kept the Law in perfect righteousness. The Rabbis therefore asked: 'Where is the Shekinah Glory of God?' The Talmud answered that the Shekinah had been driven away by Israel's sin and had therefore returned to heaven. But the Jews looked forward to the day when God's glory would return to fill the world from the central position of Zion – and this would come to pass when His kingdom came.

Righteousness is a pre-condition of the coming of the kingdom. Throughout the Old Testament God's blessing is conditional on the obedience of Israel to God's Law. In the giving of the Law it was abundantly clear that if the Jews kept God's Law they would 'live'. When God's people broke His commands and disregarded His statutes, then God turned away from them. His rule was thwarted by their sin.

Because of this both Jesus and John the Baptist preface their preaching of the kingdom with the call to repentance. A turning from sin is the prerequisite for the inauguration of the reign of God over His people. Habakkuk had foreseen that God is too pure and holy to behold evil and cannot look on wrong (Hab. 1:13). The presence of the throne of God in the midst of His people cannot coexist with iniquity – man must repent of his sin and turn to righteousness. Then it can be said that God's kingdom is at hand.

Daniel had a vision, recorded in Daniel 7, of 'one that was ancient of days' taking His seat on the throne. Then there appears the mystic figure of the Son of Man – the title which Jesus most frequently used when speaking of Himself. To the Son of Man 'was given dominion and glory and kingdom, that all peoples, nations, and languages should serve him; his dominion is an everlasting dominion . . . and his kingdom one that shall not be destroyed'. In very graphic terms Daniel also describes how this kingdom 'shall be given to the people of the saints of the Most High'. In parallel with other Old Testament pictures of the kingdom of God heralding a situation where God's people are served by other nations, Daniel sees that 'their kingdom shall be an everlasting kingdom and all dominions shall serve and obey them'. God's kingdom will be established and therefore God's people will share in His rule.

But Daniel's vision is in the context of suffering and fierce persecution. The enemy 'made war with the saints and prevailed over them until the Ancient of Days came and judgment was given for the saints of the Most High, and the time came when the saints received the kingdom' (Dn. 7 : 21, 22). Entry into the kingdom is to be prefaced by a period of trial and persecution. The Jews never lost sight of this fact – God's Word was always before them and they knew that suffering was the prelude to the blessing of the kingdom.

Under the oppression of the Roman occupation the Jews looked forward eagerly to the coming of the kingdom. Desecration of the Temple and persecution of the righteous must surely give way to the coming of the kingdom of heaven and the vindication of God's people which the prophets loved to foretell. Righteousness, persecution and the coming of the kingdom of God are inseparably connected.

In Matthew's Gospel it is recorded that Jesus 'heard that

John had been arrested' and 'from that time Jesus began to preach, saying, "Repent, for the kingdom of heaven is at hand"' (Mt. 4 : 17). The fact of John's arrest by Herod was to Jesus a sign that the kingdom was in fact at hand. Its coming was signalled by this event. Jesus knew that the prophetic word had to be fulfilled – suffering had to come before the kingdom could be inaugurated. That was one reason why in the immediately preceding verses we read that Jesus had rejected the Devil's suggestion in the wilderness that there could be an easy short-cut to 'the kingdoms of the world and the glory of them'.

The New Testament continues this same biblical picture of the necessity of suffering as a prelude to the fulfilment of the kingdom. 'There will be such tribulation as has not been from the beginning of the creation. . . . But in those days, after that tribulation, the sun will be darkened and the moon will not give its light. . . . And then they will see the Son of man coming with great power and glory' (Mark 13); and all that will come in the context of wars (verse 12) and sacrilege (verse 14). The Book of Revelation also describes most vividly the fearful battles and raging persecution which come before the final triumph of the Lamb, when the saints shall share in the glory of His Throne.

It is not surprising that persecuted Christians in Communist countries and elsewhere have often turned with renewed joy to the Book of Revelation, and discovered afresh that their suffering is not endless and hopeless. Darkness precedes light; suffering precedes joy; oppression precedes the glory of the kingdom of God.

The task of mission cannot therefore be undertaken lightly. In the last days it is bound to be in the context of distressing and fearful opposition and pain. We ourselves cannot expect an easy panacea of simple, peaceful happiness and prosperity; a baptism of fire will come upon those who side with the saints and with the Lord – only then can the kingdom come and God's rule begin.

This biblical perspective of the kingdom of heaven must, of course, influence the content both of our evangelistic preaching and of our teaching of God's church. 'Blessed are those who are persecuted for righteousness' sake, for theirs is the kingdom of heaven,' Jesus says in Matthew 5:10, 'Blessed are you when men revile you and persecute you and utter all kinds of evil against you falsely on my account. Rejoice and be glad, for your reward is great in heaven.' That is the context of the much-quoted verses about the role of Christians as salt and light in the world. Righteousness, persecution and the rewards of the kingdom of heaven go together.

The emphasis on righteousness led the Jews to expect that God would purge Israel of all ungodliness and all ungodly people at the coming of the kingdom. But the Jews were to be disappointed. The expected miracle of purging from sin did not come to pass at the outset of the kingdom; it will be perfected only when the kingdom is fulfilled at the end of time. Peter saw this clearly when he wrote in 2 Peter 3: 'We wait for new heavens and a new earth in which righteousness dwells. Therefore, beloved, since you wait for these, be zealous to be found by him without spot or blemish.' Jesus specifically taught His disciples that sin and righteousness would coexist until the close of the age. The parable of the wheat and tares is of vital significance in this respect.

Both as individuals and as churches we often long for utter purity. The individual may search for simplistic short-cuts which seem to guarantee a quick solution to the inner battle between sin and the righteousness of the indwelling Holy Spirit. As churches we may seek to guard our membership from any who are not strong in faith and pure in life. But all these attempts are in vain. The tares continue to find their way into the field of wheat.

Finally, however, the perfect kingdom will be characterized by righteousness. It is the task of mission to work for the coming of that kingdom.

3 Justice

Kittel's *Wordbook* points out that the kingdom belongs to the poor and persecuted and to children: 'of such is the kingdom of heaven'. God's kingdom is characterized not only by moral righteousness, but also by social justice. The kingdom of God is not merely a matter of individual sanctification, but also of communal justice. We are to be part of our community and to show forth the justice which ought to underlie the true community.

The Mexican theologian Miranda in his book *Marx and the Bible* rightly argues that justice and righteousness must go together. Man cannot be called righteous if he is not living in justice towards his neighbour. Both the Law and the Prophets are deeply concerned with justice in Israel. Miranda suggests that the Law was in fact introduced not to support the *status quo* with a rigid set of statutes, but rather to protect the weak and the poor. The prophets bitterly attacked the rich who oppressed the defenceless and the poor. The accumulation of wealth and power at the expense of one's fellow citizen was bitingly denounced by Amos and the other prophets. The Old Testament is vitally interested in the welfare of the fatherless, the widow and the unprotected alien within the gates of Israel. God's passionate concern for justice is a recurrent theme throughout the Old Testament.

Even the Sabbath Law was given to Israel not just for her own sake, but also for the benefit of the alien servants within the land of Israel. The seventh day was to be a day of rest so that 'the sojourner who is within your gates' and 'your manservant and your maidservant may rest as well as you. You shall remember that you were a servant in the land of Egypt' (Dt. 5 : 14, 15). Today, if a Gentile visits the home of an orthodox Jew on the Sabbath, he will be asked to do any needed small jobs like shopping or turning on the light. The Jew will be unaware that the Sabbath was given in order that the Gentile and the servant might have a day of rest too! God looks for justice in His giving of the Law.

The very name Jehovah was revealed to Moses in the context of God's heartfelt sympathy for His oppressed people and His determination to deliver them from Egyptian injustice. 'I have heard the groaning of the people of Israel whom the Egyptians hold in bondage. . . . I will deliver you from their bondage . . . with great acts of judgment' (Ex. 6).

God's deliverance of His people from oppression became the central theme of Jewish history. This story has been handed down from father to son in every Jewish family ever since.

The Jews had been cruelly treated in Egypt with all the injustice of slavery. When Israel came into the land of Canaan and developed her own state, it was clear that she was not to imitate the Egyptians by oppressing others. Israel was to be a land of justice. Gross inequality, judicial corruption, heedless carelessness towards the poor – all such injustice was attacked by the prophets. The theocratic kingdom of Israel was to be characterized by true justice.

In the Old Testament, therefore, justice is essentially within the covenant people of God. But this demonstration of justice in the theocracy was part of their task to display in communal life the glory of God, in order that the world might see and believe.

Jesus fulfilled this calling of Israel to demonstrate divine justice. He loved the widow, the sick and the outcasts of Israel. He would surely have agreed wholeheartedly with John the Baptist's words in answer to the question, 'What then shall we do?' John told the man with two coats to share with him who had none; the tax collector to collect no more than was appointed; the soldiers to rob no-one by violence or by false accusation – and to be content with their wages (Luke 3 : 10–14).

Jesus' death was, by cruel irony, the result of gross injustice. 'He died, the just for the unjust.'

The New Testament church followed the example of its Master. In the Book of Acts we read of the care of Christians for their widows, and of how they shared all that they had in order that no-one should be in want. There was to be no gross inequality either between individuals or between churches. Poor people and poor churches were helped by the generous giving of other Christians.

But again we notice that the basic arena for justice was within the covenant people of God. We saw that in the Old Testament justice was primarily within the ranks of Israel, although it also extended outwards to their neighbours. In the New Testament justice is primarily exercised within the fellowship of the church and is to be a vital part of true *koinonia*. But this life of justice also reaches out beyond the confines of the church in love for our neighbour. The command to love the brethren is extended by the command to love our neighbour as ourselves.

The fellowship of the church with its life of righteousness and justice is to be part of the mission of the church. The wonder and glory of God is demonstrated in this way, and thus He draws men to Himself. As they see the outworking of this justice they will want to submit to the authority and rule of God in His kingdom. And as, in their turn, they come by new birth into the kingdom, so they will be given the Holy Spirit who will enable them also to live in growing righteousness and justice. So the kingdom grows.

John begins his first Epistle by saying that he and his fellow witnesses testify to what they have seen and heard 'so that you may have fellowship with us; and our fellowship is with the Father and with His Son Jesus Christ'. We Christians long for all men to share in the wonders of our God-given fellowship where justice begins to be demonstrated.

4 Peace

As Christians we look forward to that great day when the tensions and antipathies of this world will finally be removed. The day will come when swords will be beaten into ploughshares and spears into pruning hooks. In this century of violence how we long for that time when 'nation shall not lift up sword against nation, neither shall they learn war any more' (Is. 2 : 4). Isaiah links the message of 'your God reigns' to the bringing of good tidings of peace (Is. 52 : 7).

Israel knew throughout her history that a right relationship with her God brought peace in its train; likewise the reign of evil in the national life always brought war and defeat. Man can enjoy peace only when he is in a right relationship of peace with his God.

'Therefore, since we are justified by faith, we have peace with God through our Lord Jesus Christ' (Rom. 5 : 1). The basis and origin of our peace must be because we have been justified through the death of Jesus Christ. In Him and in His atoning death our sin is cleansed and our broken relationship with God is restored. By His death for us Christ justifies us; He no longer reckons us to be under the curse of sin, but gives us the legal status of righteous. Thus we can know God and live at peace with Him.

There can be no peace in ourselves or in our national community without this primary foundation of peace with God Himself through Christ. The Old Testament picture of peace always assumes that we are under the rule of God and therefore at peace with Him. But peace with God is never merely a selfish and purely personal relationship with Him as our Father – it always produces a communal peace within the people of God, which also affects our attitudes to the world beyond. The climax of this growing peace at all levels will be in the perfect kingdom.

But the first outworking of the peace of God will be inner peace. Martin Buber with characteristic insight into the Jewish mind stresses that the Jew is constantly longing for and striving after an inner peace. Man is deeply uncomfortable because of the inner turmoil which results from tensions within him. This inner struggle becomes more intense when he becomes a Christian. Paul describes this experience of conflict in Romans 7 as the old nature fighting with the newly regenerate nature. Christ warned His disciples that He was coming not just to bring peace, but also to bring a sword. But this inner battle does not preclude a growing sense of deep peace which comes from the victory of the Spirit over our old nature – and that issues from a restful trust in the fact that God loves us, cares for us and will work out His purposes in us and for us.

In Ephesians 2 Paul has been writing about the reconciling work of Christ. He goes on to show that, through the cross, God 'has broken down the dividing wall of hostility. . . . He is our peace, who has made us both one'. The fact that we are at peace with God also means that we become united with each other in a new bond of love and brotherhood. Much of the New Testament is written to show that in Christ the Jew and the Gentile are now one. The peace of God breaks down the barriers that divide man. As the song says,

'We are one in the Spirit, we are one in the Lord.'

The following words of that song reflect two further aspects of this truth:

'And we pray that our unity will one day be restored'

– here is the paradox: we are already one in Christ and yet our unity is far from perfect at this stage, so we look forward to the great day when our unity will be restored.

'And they'll know we are Christians by our love'

– the loving peace of the Christian church should demonstrate the glory of God and so play a vital part in our mission.

Disunity in the ranks of God's people is not only a scandal which greatly displeases the Lord Himself, but it is also one cause of decline generally. The separation of the northern kingdom of Israel from the two tribes of the south left Israel weak both spiritually and materially. It led inevitably to the total decline of the people of God. Jesus spoke with wisdom when He said that a divided kingdom cannot stand. It is no wonder that Paul was so concerned at the disunity in the Corinthian church; or that he urged the two Philippian ladies to stop their quarrel: 'I entreat Euodia and I entreat Syntyche to agree in the Lord' (Phil. 4 : 2). Paul did not view this as just a little disagreement, but as a fundamental break in the peace of God's church.

God's peace within the church is also to reach out towards the outside world, and Paul commands the Romans, 'If possible, so far as it depends upon you, live peaceably with all' (12 : 18).

The growing kingdom

It is significant that the parables of the kingdom in Mark 4 and Matthew start with the Parable of the Sower and 'the word of the kingdom'; in Luke's Gospel also the Parable of the Sower precedes the record of the other kingdom

42

parables. The kingdom and its King are to be proclaimed.

We have seen that the kingdom of God is to be universal, but in fact its spread has not yet extended to all peoples. Likewise it is to be a kingdom of righteousness, justice and peace – but again we have already observed that these qualities are at present far from fully developed in the people of God.

The Jews expected the kingdom to arrive suddenly through the intervention of God and His Messiah. But actually the divine work of salvation comes one step at a time. The early chapters of Genesis show that God began His saving work at the dawn of history and brought it to a first stage of climax in the Exodus. He continued His salvation in the return from exile – and this is why Isaiah is happy to call the heathen king Cyrus 'God's anointed one', the Messiah. God's work takes a further great leap forward in the first coming of Jesus in humility and weakness, and it will be completed at His Second Coming. John the Baptist and Jesus Himself both say that now with the coming of Jesus the kingdom is at hand and the times are fulfilled, but it was just the start of the fulfilment of God's kingdom – the kingdom will not be complete until the end time.

The Jewish expectation of a sudden, dramatic intervention of God to bring in His kingdom is repeated in the New Testament, but now it is in respect of the final climax of the Second Coming.

Jesus taught carefully in His parables that the kingdom grows gradually. The kingdom is like a seed which grows little by little; it is like leaven which finally leavens the whole lump. Small beginnings lead to great outworkings. The kingdom is here amongst us, but yet we still pray earnestly that it will come. This is equally true of every aspect of the Christian life. We have been saved, but we look forward to our future perfect salvation. We know God, and yet we look forward to that day when we shall see the Lord and know Him even as we are known by Him. We all echo the words: 'I believe; help my unbelief.'

The joy of possession is tempered with eager anticipation of greater things to come. The Christian life may be likened to a child measuring himself against his father. The child proudly rejoices that he is now right up to his father's shoulder, but he longs for the day when he will be as tall as his father. Both as individuals and as the church of God we rejoice in that measure of the reign of God which we already enjoy, but we are also 'straining forward to what lies ahead' (Phil. 3 : 13).

God's purpose is to establish His kingdom of righteousness, justice and peace among all peoples and nations. We rejoice in the way His kingdom has spread over the centuries and at what He has done in His church to begin to fashion us in His image by the work of His Spirit. But we long for all men everywhere to submit in repentance and faith to the rule of God; we long for the new heaven and the new earth where perfect righteousness, justice and peace will be seen. The mission of the church is set in this context: we work and pray that His kingdom may come and that His will may be done on earth even as it is in heaven. And we work and pray on the basis of our assurance that 'Thine is the kingdom, the power and the glory'.

Jesus Christ is the centre of the kingdom

A comparison of Matthew 20 : 21 and Mark 10 : 37 shows that the words 'kingdom' and 'glory' are sometimes interchangeable. The glory of God is the very presence of God with His people. The kingdom of God is where God is present and reigns. When God comes into the world in the person of His Son, man can say, 'We have beheld his glory, glory as of the only Son from the Father' (Jn 1 : 14). In the person of Jesus, the Messiah, God's Shekinah glory is again present in the midst of his people. Despite the sin of Israel the Shekinah is not driven away from the world, but is again here on earth.

The Jews were looking more for the coming kingdom than for the Messiah. They thought the Messiah was merely the herald who would usher in the kingdom. But Jesus was more than a mere herald – He was the Son of Man whom Daniel had foreseen. He was also the Suffering Servant of Isaiah. The Jews had little idea of such a fulfilment of their own Old

Testament scriptures. They failed to realize that the Messiah would Himself be the glory of God; and they failed to see that this divine Messiah would come in humility and suffer on a cross for the sin of man.

The Jewish expectations of God's glory to be revealed in the coming kingdom were realized in the person of Jesus. Therefore the New Testament changes the initial message of John the Baptist and of Jesus. They came preaching the kingdom, but this quickly changed into the preaching of the person of Christ Himself. The call of the disciples was not to enter the kingdom – it was the call of Jesus, 'follow me'. He is the central figure of the kingdom. After His death and resurrection the apostles did not preach the kingdom – they preached Christ and His cross. And finally in the fulness of the heavenly kingdom the worship, honour and glory will be given to Jesus, the Lamb of God.

The message of mission must therefore remain Christ-centred. 'Follow Me' continues to be the call of Christ. In discipleship to Christ we enter the kingdom of God. We follow Him in utter submission to the Will of God; we follow Him in holiness because He is our righteousness; we follow Him in His compassionate justice and concern for the weak and the outcast; we follow Him who assures us, 'My peace I give to you'.

We remember, too, that the kingdom is connected with suffering. We are therefore not surprised when Jesus appeals to us to follow Him in taking up our cross. But this suffering of Christ has a saving and renewing purpose for men. The Christian also is called to be willing to suffer, so that the salvation of Christ may be spread to those who are still outside His kingdom.

5 Chucked out or rotting

From the outset of His ministry Jesus had in mind the plan of God for the wider international outreach of His church. When He called His disciples to follow Him, His immediate command to them was to go out to preach. During His lifetime they were to 'go nowhere among the Gentiles and enter no town of the Samaritans, but go rather to the lost sheep of the house of Israel'; but right from the outset of their discipleship they were to go out and preach. The training had begun.

What task were the disciples called to fulfil? In Mark 3 it is shown to be a threefold commission. They were to be with the Lord for teaching and fellowship; they were to be sent out to preach; and they were to have authority to cast out demons.

It is often thought that the disciples had three years of instruction in fellowship with the incarnate Jesus and only then did they move out into the active evangelism that we see in the Book of Acts. This is not a correct picture. Their three years of discipleship before the death of Jesus were a period of constant change. They had times when they were 'with Him' and then times when they were out in society at large preaching and working. This was the way Jesus trained them: times of withdrawal for teaching and fellowship were interspersed with times of practical experience in the wider world. It is also a pattern for the life of any Christian. All of us need times of withdrawal from the pressures of the world, so that we can be 'with Him'. And all disciples of Christ are also called to an out-going ministry where they are 'sent out' into society.

If a Christian is to be sent out into the battle-field of the world, he needs to be equipped for spiritual warfare. Christ gave His disciples authority to cast out demons. The Christian today is likewise equipped for a life of victory over Satan and all his works. What this means becomes clear in the Great Commission in Matthew 28, where the Christian is commanded to 'go and make disciples' because he is first assured that 'all authority in heaven and on earth has been given' to the Christ who now dwells by His Spirit in us. With this assured power within us we are able to 'go and make disciples of all nations'.

It is significant that the original call of the twelve disciples, recorded in Mark 3, is very similar to that final command of Jesus in Matthew 28. His call and commission to His disciples never changed – and it is still the same today.

Jesus called the twelve to be with Him in Mark 3 and in Matthew 28 He promised to be with them always. In Mark 3 He sent them out to preach and in Matthew 28 they are commanded to go and make disciples of all nations. In Mark 3 He gave them authority to cast out demons, while in Matthew 28 He assured them that in Him was vested all authority.

When Jesus calls men to Himself as His disciples, His desire and command for them is always that they should enjoy fellowship and teaching 'with Him', that they should be sent out to preach, and also that they should go with the assurance of His authority in them over Satan and all his powers. This was true of His disciples in the first century and it remains true today.

In Luke 9 we see an example of Jesus' training of His disciples for this task. They had evidently had a time away from Jesus, but now He 'called the twelve together'. Having given them 'power and authority over all demons and to cure diseases . . . he sent them out to preach the kingdom of God and to heal'. So after a short time together with Jesus, the twelve are sent out again into active service to preach and heal.

Twelve men for the whole land of Israel is hardly an adequate missionary force. We are therefore not surprised when we read in the following chapter that 'after this the Lord appointed seventy others, and sent them'. They too went out with the same commission to preach and to heal; they too had the same assurance that the demons would be subject to them in Jesus' name.

It is in this context of active missionary work that Jesus tells His followers to pray for labourers. 'The harvest is plentiful, but the labourers are few,' He informed them. They knew it already from experience – they were working in the whole land of Israel and even with the new reinforcements of the 'seventy others' the number of missionaries was pitifully insufficient. Doubtless in their hearts they echoed a meaningful 'Amen' when Jesus reminded them that 'the labourers are few'. (Yet today there are many areas of the world far larger than Israel with even less adequate numbers of missionary personnel.) Therefore, exhorts Jesus, 'pray . . . the Lord of the harvest to send out labourers into his harvest'. The prayer that the Lord will thrust out labourers must always be in the context of active evangelistic witness on the part of the man who prays. Only in this way will the prayer truly come from the heart; and only if it comes from the heart will it be effective.

When we are in the cosy atmosphere of a large Christian fellowship, the desperate need for missionary workers is hardly borne in upon us. But when we begin to witness in the spiritually lonely situation of a factory, hospital or college, then we begin to sense personally the need for the Lord to send more labourers into His harvest. We feel our real weakness in the midst of a mass of non-Christians, and we cry to the Lord for reinforcements.

But often the reinforcements don't want to come. Few Christians really want to be thrust out into the harvest, into active witness in the world. It is so much easier to remain inactive and to enjoy the fellowship of the church: life in the world is much harder. Few of us want to be sent even to those immediately around us, let alone be involved in mission overseas. Jesus therefore commands His people to pray the Lord to 'send out' labourers. Our Bible translations are perhaps a little too polite here. The Greek word

48

means not 'send out', but 'throw out'. This was a violent word which was used for the throwing out of rubbish. In those days, of course, there were no refuse disposal services. If one had some inoffensive rubbish which was unlikely to become unduly noxious, it was the custom to drop it gently from the window and allow it to rot beneath the house. But if one had a piece of rubbish which would develop an unpleasant smell, then one went up to the house-top, flexed one's muscles and hurled the offending article as far as one could from the house. It is this violent word for the throwing out of rubbish which is used in this passage. We are to pray the Lord of the harvest that He will hurl out labourers; perhaps 'kick out' or 'chuck out' might be more apt translations.

We are not suggesting that all missionaries or active witnesses for Christ are to be compared with offensive rubbish! But it is true that most of us are unwilling to be called out into the Lord's service and are therefore in need of God's more violent working in us. Many a missionary's testimony tells of this: 'I was happy to do anything for the Lord, but I had no intention of becoming a missionary. But the Lord so worked in me that finally I just had to say to Him, "All right, Lord, I'll go if you want". Then came the Lord's confirming peace of heart.'

Even the apostles Peter and Paul needed a strong push from the Lord. Only then were they happy to be involved in the wider mission beyond their own Jewish people to the Gentiles.

Both of them were already active in witness among their own people. But Peter needed that vision of the unclean animals in the sheet before he was ready to respond to God's initiative in sending him to Cornelius. Even Paul did not find Gentile mission easy. At Paul's conversion God told Ananias that Paul was a chosen instrument to carry God's name before the Gentiles. Ananias therefore told Paul that he was to be a 'witness to all men'. Immediately after this Paul went up to Jerusalem and there God appeared to him in a trance, saying, 'depart, for I will send you far away to the Gentiles'. Despite these clear instructions Paul needed to be 'thrust out' into witness to Gentiles. It was at least ten years before this happened, in Antioch of Pisidia, as described in Acts 13.

Paul began his work in Antioch by preaching in the synagogue, where large numbers of Jews became interested in the gospel and some even believed. They begged him to preach there again on the next Sabbath. During the intervening week the news had spread – an exciting new preacher with a soul-stirring message of the Messiah had come to Antioch. Gentiles as well as Jews were fascinated and 'the next sabbath almost the whole city gathered together to hear the word of God'. Was Paul's message to be preached now to Gentiles as well as to Jews? The Jews were filled with jealousy when they saw the massed crowds and they began to stir up opposition. So God moved Paul to 'turn to the Gentiles'. The eager, open hearts of the Gentiles combined with the bitter opposition of the Jews to force his hand – he had no choice but to minister to Gentiles. He spoke boldly to the Jews present: 'It was necessary that the word of God should be spoken first to you. Since you thrust it from you, and judge yourselves unworthy of eternal life, behold, we turn to the Gentiles.' And this reminded Paul himself of his original calling through Ananias to this wider ministry beyond the confines of his own people. He added, 'For so the Lord has commanded us, saying, "I have set you to be a light for the Gentiles, that you may bring salvation to the uttermost parts of the earth".'

Thanks to their earlier preparation by Jesus, the apostles found no problems in going to the Samaritans. In Acts 8 the church of Jerusalem was scattered throughout Samaria and Philip went down there and 'proclaimed to them the Christ'. The door to the Samaritans had been opened. And now the way was equally open for outreach to Gentiles. Peter's vision and Paul's experiences in Antioch had pushed open that door too.

Before He ascended to heaven Jesus told His disciples, 'You shall receive power when the Holy Spirit has come upon you; and you shall be my witnesses in Jerusalem and in all Judea and Samaria and to the end of the earth.' To

Jews? Yes! To Samaritans? Yes! To Gentiles? At last, yes! To the end of the earth? Not yet. The history of the outreach of the church was just beginning.

Pentecost and mission go together. The selection and call of the apostles to the wider proclamation of the gospel was the task of the Holy Spirit. Thus in Acts 13 it is the Holy Spirit who says: 'Set apart for me Barnabas and Saul for the work to which I have called them.' The Holy Spirit not only calls men to mission, but also then empowers them in their preaching and gives them the spiritual gifts they need for their ministry. It is the work of the Holy Spirit when the power of the preacher is matched by the receptivity of the listeners – He works in their hearts and minds to convince them of sin, righteousness and judgment. So the ultimate purpose of the Spirit is fulfilled – Jesus Christ is uplifted and glorified. In the Book of Acts the over-all strategy and timing of the apostles' missionary outreach is directed by the Spirit.

The Book of Acts is not a textbook for doctrine: if one wants to study the doctrinal truths of the Christian faith, one does not turn to this book of history. Acts shows the working of God the Holy Spirit in the expansion and development of the church. Acts is a book of mission. Nor is church history primarily for the study of systematic theology: in it we are to see the working of God in the ever-widening outreach of His people. It is to be regretted that church history is too often taught from the point of view of theology.

The first few hundred years of the Christian church are commonly associated with a series of doctrinal battles over the definition of the Trinity. We study the findings of the various church councils and contrast the heresies of the Arians and others. The development of theological definitions is important; we have also much to learn from the heretical mistakes of the past. But church history shows above all the development of mission as the church reaches out into ever-widening circles. How much do we know of how the gospel spread around the Mediterranean lands? We know that those early doctrinal battles were fought partly by men of God from Alexandria and from Hippo in North Africa. But how did the gospel ever penetrate these places? Later we find a church council in Arles in Gaul: but how did the gospel shine into the darkness of the French tribes? The study of mission in those early days is a rewarding task. God's working by His Spirit in the outreach of His church is always stimulating to faith and challenging to dedication.

The period of the church's history from AD 450 to about AD 1450 is usually called the Dark Ages. Perhaps this is not only because of the spiritual darkness that often prevailed then, but also because we are so often in the dark about that period. It happens to be the era when most of Europe was brought into the church of Christ; not therefore an altogether fruitless time in terms of mission! Our ignorance of this period of history means that we know little of the evangelization of our own land or of other areas of Europe. This in turn may strengthen mistaken views of the Christian faith as a European religion, for we forget that Europe had to be evangelized and won from its tribal paganism. Many centuries elapsed before Christianity gained the upper hand throughout Europe – and we know today how easily the former pagan beliefs reassert themselves. The conversion of Europe was never complete; Europe today is as much in need of mission as any other continent.

The brave faith of those early missionaries to Britain and the rest of Europe would move us to a new determination to follow the Lord and be His ambassadors throughout the world – but sadly we are not taught about them. The Yorkshireman is proud of his current sporting heroes, but he is often ignorant of those pioneer missionaries who dared all to bring the gospel to his savage tribal forefathers. What an epic tale it is of the missionaries who ventured across the wild fens into East Anglia! Those centuries may be a dark age for theology, but God had His own men of faith to continue the unfinished story of the Book of Acts. The Holy Spirit still empowered men to be Christ's witnesses 'to the end of the earth'.

Britain was not only a mission-field: it was also sending

missionaries across the waters to Europe. Boniface left the shores of Britain to do battle with the pagans of Germany and Holland. Based on Fulda in the heart of what is now West Germany, he travelled widely to preach Christ to the various tribal groups. Churches were founded and men won for Christ. He pushed through the wolf-infested forests of Germany to take the gospel to the barbaric Frisians in what is now Holland. Here he met the death of a martyr, vainly defending his head from their sharp knives with a book. Through Boniface and others who followed in his footsteps God changed lives. The fundamental nature of a people was changed by the power of God's Spirit.

After the Dark Ages one returns with a sigh of relief to the more familiar territory of the Reformation and its theological battles concerning justification by faith and also the authority of Scripture. This immensely important time in the life of God's church was to have a fundamental influence on the whole development of Christianity, including its missionary outreach. One has only to compare the missionary approaches of Catholic and Protestant missions to see how their varying doctrinal beliefs have affected the strategy of their work. There seems little similarity between Catholic missionary methods in Latin America or the Philippines and the work of such Protestant pioneers as Carey, Judson or Hudson Taylor.

Internecine battles in the British church led to such persecution that Christians fled across the Atlantic and so the gospel spread in the North American continent. Likewise a questionable British policy towards Australia resulted inadvertently in the establishment of churches in that great continent. These early churches in America and Australasia brought the gospel of Jesus Christ to the Indian and Aboriginal populations and later were the instrument of God for widespread mission in other countries. Today 70% of Protestant missionaries are from North America.

Despite the internal weaknesses of the church and therefore the inevitable traumatic disputes and even divisions, God carried forward His purposes for the nations of the world. He continued to push His people out into new areas with the gospel, and the name of Jesus Christ came to be worshipped by people of an ever-increasing multitude of nations and tongues. Catholic and Orthodox missions continued to reach out into their respective areas of influence. Later they were joined by a great host of Protestant missions, many of which were inspired by the various revival movements in Europe and America.

Relations between the different missions were not always of the best. Rivalry and resentment often embittered their members and spoilt their testimony. Sometimes they were moved to new pioneer outreach from a wrong desire to beat their rival mission! Sometimes too there were other wrong motives connected with colonialism and power; but God nevertheless continued to use earthen vessels to bring His glory to men and women. The church continued to move out to all the earth.

The Bible looks forward to the climax of God's kingdom, when the Lamb will be worshipped by 'a great multitude which no man could number, from every nation, from all tribes and peoples and tongues'. God's plan of salvation is that people from all nations should come to repentance and life-giving faith. His disciples are to go to 'the end of the earth', and only then will the climax of Christ's Second Coming take place. Peter (2 Pet. 3:12) exhorts his readers not only to wait patiently for 'the coming of the day of God', but also to hasten it. The Christian is to play his part under God in bringing about the necessary pre-conditions for that great culmination of history when Christ shall come and the kingdom of the Messiah shall be fulfilled. One of the pre-conditions is that there shall be people from every nation, tribe, people and tongue who have become Christ's disciples and who will therefore worship Him in the kingdom. Therefore Christ commands His disciples, 'Go and make disciples of all nations'.

6 To all the people

'Would you give your testimony in the Youth Meeting next week?' I asked a young Chinese girl in Malaysia. She was a quiet girl who rarely took part in conversation. Her parents and brother had also been converted several years before and as a family they had grown as Christians. Her brother was gifted and out-going with a real ability for leading singing. There were so many talented young people in the church that she felt overwhelmed and shy. Others seemed to grow so quickly in their Christian life and their Christian character was obvious.

My question shocked her. What sort of testimony could she give? What evidence was there of spiritual life and growth? No, she could not and would not stand up in front of all those other people to give her testimony.

'Have you been converted?' I asked with the aim of encouraging her confidence. Her answer was a clear 'Yes'. 'Has God done anything in you to change your life since you came out of Buddhism?' The girl answered without hesitation – the Lord had done so much to help her. But still she doubted whether she really had any gifts to be used for Him.

I knew that much of the life of the church often depended on this one girl, for quietly and efficiently she did so much of the work behind the scenes. If there was anything practical to be done in the church, she could be depended upon not only to start it but also to complete the job. So many other people would begin doing things, but sometimes were side-tracked from finishing them.

The girl had never before realized the importance of the

part she played in the working of the body of Christ in that town. 'So I do have gifts,' she exclaimed, 'and the Lord has made me useful.' She did not give her testimony publicly – she would not have felt at ease in such ministry anyway – but this conversation helped her to a wider appreciation of the varying gifts of God.

She was a girl who could be trusted to do a piece of work efficiently and to finish the work she began. This is the very character of God being worked out in the life of one of His children. God's nature is to complete whatever work He begins. The Christian is comforted by the assurance that 'He who began a good work in you will bring it to completion'. God is not content only with the new birth of the Christian, but wants also to sanctify him and bring him to maturity. Babies are beautiful and admired by all, but twenty-year-old babies are a sad sight.

As this is true of God's work in the individual, so it is true also of His work on a broader front. God is not content with the planting of the church among a people; He wants His church to be edified, matured and perfected.

In John 4 : 34 Jesus said, 'my food is to do the will of him who sent me, and to accomplish his work'. What does He mean by 'my food'? Perhaps the nearest equivalent is 'my meat and drink' – my longing, the one thing I desire, my ambition. Here Jesus describes His over-riding ambition. In these words we see unveiled the motivation behind His whole life and work.

The Christian claims that Jesus lives in him by the Holy Spirit. At our conversion we asked Jesus to come into our lives. Since He does now live in us, something of the character and desires of Jesus should be forming in us. We should begin to think the thoughts of Jesus. Paul says with disarming simplicity, 'we have the mind of Christ'. What a bold claim! If it is true, the great ambition in the life of Jesus ought also to motivate His followers. If Jesus longs 'to do the will of him who sent me, and to accomplish his work', then this same longing should be forming in the heart of the Christian who is indwelt by Christ.

'To do' and 'to accomplish' – what do these words mean?

What is meant by doing the will of God? Peter says the Lord wishes 'that all should reach repentance'. Paul says that God 'desires all men to be saved and to come to the knowledge of the truth'. God's will must therefore include his desire that the life-giving knowledge of the truth in Christ should be taken to all men everywhere, so that men of all races may be able to respond in repentance and faith. The will of God therefore involves an out-going evangelism.

Paul also says, 'this is the will of God, your sanctification'. Here he is addressing the whole Thessalonian church, not just an individual. God wants the whole church to be sanctified as a body. This naturally includes a growing holiness in the life of each member of the body, but it goes further than that. God's ambition is that the whole church should become increasingly Christ-like. God is not satisfied with evangelism only – He wants to see His church built up into the image of God, into the character of Christ. In this way the will of God is 'accomplished'.

In the centre of God's will, then, are two elements: evangelism and the edification of the resultant church. Jesus puts it very simply at the end of Matthew's Gospel. He commands His disciples not only to 'go and make disciples of all nations', but also to baptize them and thus form living churches. Jesus goes on to give a third command: they are also to 'teach them to observe all that I have commanded you'. Evangelism, church-planting and then the teaching of the church – these things are the will of God. They are also vital to mission.

We must now look in more detail at some specific situations in the world today with regard to each of these three elements of the will of God.

Evangelism

The task of the church is to take the message of Christ to every race and nation, to every segment of the population. Pioneer evangelism today falls into three categories. It may mean taking the gospel to an area of a country which is as yet unevangelized. It may mean going to a racial group which is as yet untouched by the love of Christ. Or it may mean outreach into a social class or segment of the population which is still outside the kingdom of Christ.

A new area

I was bumping along on a rough lorry through the arid, flat countryside of East Thailand on my way to the little country of Laos. It was the height of the dry season and the journey was hot and dusty. Later the dead fields would come alive with a spurt of fresh green life when the rains descended and coaxed the rice up into luxuriant beauty. But now everything was blanketed in a thick layer of brown dust which flew up into my nostrils. The pot-holed road did not add to the comfort, as the lorry lurched and jolted its way eastwards hour by hour.

We drove through village after village, small town after small town. It was largely a rural area, with scattered hamlets all along the road. Traditional Thai Buddhism with its strong animistic background reigned unchallenged. From a Christian point of view this was an unevangelized area, and my heart was deeply moved. It is easy to talk lightly of the need for pioneer evangelism in 'unreached areas' when one is living in a country sated with a form of Christianity which often lacks reality and life. But when a Christian travels through a huge area with a population ignorant of the Christ who can meet their needs, then the pathos of those words 'the unevangelized' hits home.

Eighty-two per cent of the population of India is rural; yet most of the churches are in the cities. The country areas are strongly Hindu. In the West we think of Hinduism as a high and mystic philosophy. This appeals to current trends in western thought which reject the concept of the absolute and react against religious intolerance. But in fact only the upper castes follow this type of Hinduism. In the villages polytheistic worship largely prevails. This latter form of Hinduism owes much to earlier Aryan religion which offered propitiatory sacrifices to a profusion of nature gods. To this was added later the worship of the divine incarnations, like Krishna, which emerge so vividly in the Upanishad literature. The rural areas of India with their popular Hindu beliefs, as well as the bigger cities with their higher religious philosophy, both stand in need of the living Christ, the way to the one Father.

This need of evangelism in rural society could be paralleled in many countries. It is particularly poignant in the Muslim world of the Middle East and North Africa; but all over the world there remains much pioneer mission still to be done.

A new racial group

We were watching the army of bulldozers ploughing through the slippery mud. Our television was showing us the birth of the huge trans-continental highway of Brazil about which we had read so much. Within the space of a few years the whole Amazon valley will be opened up to the influences of 'civilization'. What will this mean to the isolated tribal groups who for centuries have sheltered behind dense jungle and remote mountains? Their old familiar tribal customs will melt under the onslaught of new ideas and fresh philosophies. Inevitably they will be forced to examine their way of life and traditional beliefs in the light of these new influences. They stand precariously at a dangerous crossroad in their tribal history, easily harmed, easily led. Are we in the church of Christ offering them, as we should, the only true security which can be found in this world?

Many other areas of the world have experienced the same sweeping changes when radical improvement in communications has rapidly altered the way of life. The church should be pressing forward to enter these new doors of opportunity.

Christians believe that the gospel is to be preached to all nations and that God longs for His salvation to be available to all men of all races. Even the tiny, remote tribal group has a right to know about Jesus Christ and what He can do for them.

In the last decade there has sprung up a great movement into tribal missionary work, and through this movement many new racial groups have been reached with the knowledge of Christ. The Scriptures have been translated into many new languages.

But the church's outreach among new racial groups is not only a question of tribal work. Even in big cities, where there may be several churches, there is often one race or even several races which have no Christians.

Singapore is a case in point. There are many lively churches in this flourishing modern city. Most of the churches are Chinese, though a few are made up of Indians of different language groups. Yet among the Malays, who form over 10% of the population, only a handful of Christians can be found. The Sikhs who migrated from North India are in an even worse position as they are completely unevangelized. They live largely in their own areas of the city. The Sikh community is close-knit and fiercely resistant to any Christian witness. If a Sikh becomes interested in Christ, there will be very definite persecution. Despite the presence of many live Christian churches in the city, it remains sadly true that the message of Jesus Christ has still not been brought to the Sikhs and has made little impact on the Malays.

A new social class
Here in Britain we often decry the fact that Christianity is largely a middle-class religion. Most of our larger and more lively churches are filled with people from the 'nicer' areas of suburbia together with some students. The rougher downtown areas and housing estates may well have very few Christians. Active Christians on the factory floor or down the coal mines are a tiny minority. The presence of a middle-class church near the factory or just down the road from the worker's home is irrelevant to the evangelization of the shop-floor employee. Pioneer evangelism may still be needed here.

'What do you say to people who have never heard the name of Jesus? How can you communicate the gospel to someone with no background of Christian teaching?' A little group of missionary-minded students wanted to know what missionary work was really like and they were asking me all sorts of questions. I described my feelings when I first met and talked with someone who had never before heard anything about Jesus. He was a rough semi-literate lad of about seventeen. The boy had seen a church near where he lived, but he had no idea what went on in it. Then one day we met and I talked with him about Jesus. He was baffled and could not understand what it was all about. He thought 'Jesus' was just a swear word – and now I was using the name as if Jesus were a person.

Finally it became apparent to the students that the boy I was speaking of was Welsh. The mission-field was closer than they thought! Of course there were churches where the boy had been brought up, but the Christian message had not penetrated the social circles in which he moved. Pioneer mission was needed in that particular segment of the population of Wales.

The state of Kerala in South India is noted not only for the strength of the Communists, but also for its large Christian community. The Mar Thoma churches are centred on this state. They have a large number of churches, and also an annual conference rather like the Keswick Convention. Tents are pitched throughout the area and tens of thousands gather for a week of meetings. One cannot but be impressed by these ancient churches which are said to date back to a visit to India by the Apostle Thomas in the first century. They are certainly not European in their ways and may shock us by their ritualism and formality, but God has kept and used them through the centuries. Today they too are sending missionaries to other areas and peoples.

Recently a survey was made of the membership of the churches of Kerala, and this revealed a significant failure. Virtually all the Christians in the different churches and denominations came either from the high caste or from the lowest caste. The middle castes are still unevangelized – they are solidly Hindu. Pioneer evangelism is needed even in Kerala.

In many Latin American countries the Pentecostals have made sweeping advances in the past few years. Largely because of their staggering growth, Latin America is now often quoted as an example of a very open and fruitful mission area. About 75% of all Christians in that continent are now members of one of the multitude of different Pentecostal denominations. Some 5,000 new churches emerge each year, some of them attracting huge congregations.

But Pentecostal membership is almost exclusively drawn from the down-and-out masses. Many are won for Christ in the spreading shanty towns on the edges of the large mushrooming cities. In some parts the Pentecostals have won great numbers of poor Indians. Being sufficiently flexible and far-sighted to follow the progress of the trans-continental highway across Brazil, they have founded new congregations in place after place where the road has been built.

But what about the middle and upper classes? What about the student world of Latin America? Relatively little impact is being made here. At present these social circles are the sphere of other Protestant churches and missions, for the Pentecostals have not yet succeeded in widening their scope. Much more needs to be done in pioneer evangelism in those areas and segments of society which the Pentecostals are not equipped to tackle.

Strategic opportunities for evangelism

There are three key areas which present great strategic opportunities for evangelism today – city evangelism, student evangelism and evangelism through the mass media. The church would do well to reappraise its attitude to these in its long-term planning.

City evangelism

In 1871 there were only eleven cities in the world which had a population of over a million; today there are 100. Asia alone has at least 50 such cities. Before the Communists captured it, even Phnom Penh in Cambodia had some two million inhabitants; yet this is not considered to be one of the main Asian cities. Peking, Tokyo, Manila, Bangkok, Jakarta, Hong Kong, Bombay, Calcutta – one could go on listing great Asian cities with huge populations which make a British city like Birmingham with its one million people sound quite puny.

In 1900 Latin America had only ten cities with populations of more than 100,000; today there are some 700 such cities, of which at least twelve have more than a million. The Argentinians have a proverb which says, 'God made the rest of the world in six days and saved the seventh for Rio de Janeiro'! Rio is a great city and might well be thought worthy of a whole day of creation all to itself; but today it is overtaken by even larger cities as South America becomes increasingly urbanized. The 1965 University of California statistics claim that more than 60% of the population of Uruguay, Chile, Venezuela and Argentina is urban. Since 1965 this percentage must have increased. The Evangelical Alliance report, *One World, One Task*, claims that in 1900 12% of the world's population were city dwellers; by 1971 this had increased to 40% and they estimate that by the end of the century it will be 90%. The significance of these facts must be realized in any forward-thinking missionary strategy.

Such rapid urbanization brings with it many problems. The breakdown of traditional village or tribal culture patterns together with the destruction of the extended family lead to a sense of bewilderment. People do not know how to live or what their role in society should be. They feel isolated and lonely, with little sense of community. They are also free to develop new ways of life and new philosophies, for the restraining influence of their traditional society has been lost. They are therefore open to become Christians or Marxists – or anything else which may seem to satisfy. This situation presents an urgent call to Christians to offer the Truth, Christ Himself, to those who are searching for a new way of life.

Unfortunately the Christian church in western lands has not been noted for success in evangelism in the slum areas of cities or in blocks of high-rise flats. It is in these areas however that the church overseas must make inroads, for that is where the people are. This has been part of the clue to Pentecostal growth in South America. They have succeeded in drawing into their churches the recent arrivals in the shanty towns on the edges of the cities. It is an accepted fact that new city dwellers are open to fresh ideas for the first ten to fifteen years. After that they settle down into a regular pattern of life and philosophy which is not easily shaken.

Just off the road from the airport in Singapore lies the huge new housing estate of Toa Payoh with its vast blocks of flats stretching into the sky. There is little space between the buildings. The visitor can feel overwhelmed – crowds of men, women and children jostle one another like a swarm of ants. We were informed that these blocks of flats were to house as many people as the whole of the city of Coventry. 'Jesus', Matthew says, 'saw the crowds.' When one walks in the midst of the crowds of an Asian city, one shares that sense of longing which Jesus had. 'He had compassion for them,' Matthew continues, 'because they were harassed and helpless, like sheep without a shepherd.' In such a new city situation people need a shepherd. It is not by chance that many of the dynamic new leaders in the Third World call themselves by such religious names as 'Saviour' or 'the Great Leader'.

Africans are particularly aware of this need. Dynamic prophets and prophetesses in their striking robes are an integral feature of the street scene. Circles of worshipping dancers gladly acclaim their gifted leaders. There are many reasons for the phenomenal growth of these Independency and Prophet Movements in Africa today, but surely one reason is the need for community and leadership. These movements, too, often use such messianic titles as 'Saviour' for their leaders.

As Christians we believe that there is only one Saviour of the world. We long for men and women to know and follow Him. But how can we develop a strategy which is effective in reaching the masses in the cities? When Toa Payoh was built, the government reserved one plot of land for a religious building – it would go to the highest bidder by auction. It was with a sense of dismay that the churches realized that the cost was prohibitive. This meant that there would be no church building in the whole area. But, in fact, this has turned out to be a blessing. Evangelism based on a church building is probably unsuited to large blocks of flats.

Different churches began to rent flats or to encourage

their members to live in this estate. Several 'flat churches' have evolved. Their aim is to have such centres of light on every floor of every block of flats. These homes are used not only for worship, but also for all sorts of community-developing activities. In such circumstances the church can have a ministry at every level of need, as well as in evangelism.

Missionary work in big cities does not have the romantic appeal of other forms of service. Home churches and their young people will respond to tribal, rural or medical needs more easily than to city work – that is too much like Birmingham or Leeds! But with the ever-growing number of people in the cities, we must join Jesus in having compassion for the crowds – not just for individuals or minority groups, but also for the crowds.

Student evangelism
The hunger for education is one of the great facts of our age. In each of the newly independent countries crowds of young people press into the schools, colleges and universities. In most such countries 50% or more of the population is composed of young people, and they therefore form a significant part of the nation's political voice. Over the last few years violent action by students has toppled governments in several countries. Student demonstrations are not to be laughed at as mere youthful exuberance.

Latin American sociologists constantly remind us that university students are the key segment of their countries' population. What students think this morning, the rest of the world thinks this afternoon. Even in the strongly Muslim lands the students are questioning and therefore somewhat more open than their fellow countrymen.

Buddhists have begun mission work in Britain. Where would you expect them to concentrate their efforts? In some remote country village? Of course not! The British countryside is firmly conservative in outlook and 'C of E' in religion – even if the people do not actually attend their parish church except on special occasions. The idea of our traditional country people becoming Buddhists is ludicrous. No! The Buddhists have a better sense of strategy; they began their work among students and in the more 'arty' section of Hampstead. It is in such circles that they meet people who are rebellious against the accepted norms of society and who are open to change.

Paul's strategy in the Book of Acts was similar. He went largely to the cities and to those segments of society where people were receptive to new ideas.

Missionary work among students overseas can be done in various ways. One can work full-time with a student organization like IFES or Campus Crusade (missionaries are also loaned to such movements by the various missions). It is possible to work in a missionary society and be located in a house near a University campus. The home can then be used for Bible studies, informal discussions, teaching English or any other activity which gives good contact with students. Those who are adequately qualified have a further opportunity: they can lecture on the staff of educational institutions. Missions may loan such workers to a University or college; these new missionaries will then have the benefit of their mission's help in language and cultural training. In lands where missionaries are no longer welcome, it is clearly strategic that Christians should take up such teaching posts and thus give local students the opportunity to hear for themselves and to make up their own minds what they want to believe.

Whatever means we use, it is of the utmost importance that the church should not opt out of the battle for the minds and souls of students. Communists are keen to win this particular struggle and often make considerable gains in the universities. Christians also need to be alive to the significance of the student world. The Lambeth Conference of 1948 was right when it said, 'the supreme conflict of our generation is a struggle between Christian and Marxist for the soul of man'. This conflict will largely be won or lost in the student world.

Mass media evangelism

In 1850 the world's population was only about 1,000 million. Now it is well over 3,000 million. By the end of this century it is estimated that there will be at least 7,000 million people – and it is our responsibility as Christ's ambassadors to bring His gospel to all people. If we are to do what He commands, then we shall need to use every available means. In our generation we have been given the use of a variety of mass media – literature, radio and television.

We have already noted how the world is hungry for education. Vast numbers of people are becoming literate and will read whatever is put before them in an attractive format. Again, sadly, we have to admit that the Communists are often the leaders in this field. They do not normally bother to teach people to read, but they make full use of others' literacy work by providing Communist literature for the masses to feed on.

When Indonesia won her independence after the Second World War, only about 14% of the population was reckoned to be literate. Now about 75% of the population is in the market for reading materials. It is vital that sufficient good literature be produced and distributed to meet the need of the 100 million potential readers of Indonesia. This is equally true of many other countries in each continent.

Christians need to produce such attractive literature that it can easily be sold in free competition with other books. Funds for free distribution of Bibles and other Christian books are limited. Missionaries should set an example in selling books and also in encouraging other Christians to do likewise. This ministry can be begun in Britain through our regular church meetings, home meetings, Bible study groups, and so on.

Most missionary societies require men and women who can help at every level of literature work – by writing, translating, editing, printing, managing bookshops, or working as travelling salesmen.

A key ministry overseas is to train national writers to produce Christian literature which is suited to the culture and background of the country. In the past we have depended too heavily on translated works. But these present real problems.

'We cannot use any of these books,' said the representative of a national literature committee, 'they are all foreign and imperialistic.' The committee had been given a selection of English missionary biographies; they were asked to select some for translation into their own language. Finally it was agreed that with careful editing one or two of the books could be adapted for an African readership.

Literature is a vital factor in the evangelization of the world, and also in the teaching and building up of God's church.

But literature is not the only tool at our disposal these days. Radio can often minister where missionaries are not allowed. Even where they are permitted, it may still be easier for people to listen at home to a radio programme than to take the initiative in visiting the foreigner's home or listening to the Christian message in a church. Any such move may bring fierce opposition when a man is still at the early stage of enquiry and therefore not yet ready to face persecution for Christ. He can listen secretly to the radio before committing himself to a more open interest.

Radio can be used in two ways. First there are radio stations which are clearly committed to the proclamation of the Christian faith. These are free to use every modern means of presentation to introduce the listener to Christ in an attractive way. But also one can often work through a national broadcasting station, producing programmes which are not overtly Christian but which have a Christian ethos and underlying philosophy. Every play or story on radio or television has a belief as its basis. Although this belief is not directly preached in words, yet it comes across through the story and subtly influences the listener. If the Christian can produce scripts of such quality that they are acceptable for their interest-value, then he can have a real influence through the national broadcasting system. This applies equally to television.

'Missionary television,' queried an elderly lady after an Open Day meeting at All Nations Christian College, 'whatever next? Paul never used television!' She had just heard the testimony of a young couple who were about to

68

leave the college in order to preach Christ through television overseas. The use of Christian literature and radio is now accepted in most of our churches, but few pray or give for television work.

About 98% of all homes in Japan have television. Even in Thailand four channels are beamed across the land. Particularly in the cities, but also in other areas, this is the medium which increasingly shapes the thinking of ordinary people. More and more people throughout the world are developing square eyes! The production of effective, good-quality programmes is a very expensive and exceedingly skilled task. If the programme is not of a really professional standard, it is only too easy for viewers to switch over to a different channel.

There is no need for Christians always to be the last to use modern means for the dissemination of their message. For years it was considered taboo to use films for the Lord – now it is quite normal. But films are almost out of date in the world around us; cinemas are turning into bingo halls! Today many Christians are equally suspicious of TV as being somehow satanic, whereas in fact it is surely spiritually neutral – everything depends on who uses it. Some missions in Japan especially have found it a very effective instrument for the Lord.

Tribes, rural areas, cities, students – men and women of every kind are to be reached with the gospel, and every God-given means is to be used. Evangelism is a vital part of God's call to His followers. Jesus longed to do the will of Him who sent Him; He longed to preach the kingdom of God, and it remains His great yearning that His disciples should reach out to the ends of the earth. 'Go and make disciples of all nations.'

Church planting

The task of the church is not only to preach the gospel, but also to baptize and thus to form churches. Christians are so made that they function better in fellowship. We are not meant to be lone Christians except in very exceptional circumstances. In the hostile climate of persecution which

Christians face in many countries overseas, it is doubly important that they should be part of a strong praying fellowship. Evangelism should have as its definite aim the founding and planting of churches.

Denominational churches can sometimes be too rigid in the exporting of their own particular structures, so that the churches they found overseas are just replicas of their parents. This has the advantage of producing definite and firm foundations, but the church structure may be quite unsuited to the cultural background of the people. On the other hand, interdenominational missions have had grave difficulties in finding any suitable structure for church life which could be agreed by all the varying members of the mission. They have tended, therefore, to found churches with an indefinite church order, but which approximate to a Baptist or independent church in the home country. Conferences of interdenominational missions often have long discussions about the details of church structures – do you appoint elders before deacons, or vice versa? Are elders appointed for an indefinite period or for a limited number of years? Who chooses elders and deacons?

When Wesley went to America as a pioneer missionary, he was in some ways remarkably naïve. He looked forward to discovering from the American Indians the genuine interpretation of Scripture on all subjects. He felt that with their lack of Christian tradition the Indians would inevitably find the true meaning of the Bible. Bitter disappointment awaited him. The Indians either found themselves unable to interpret the Bible at all and therefore looked for guidance from the missionary, or they interpreted it from the point of view of their own cultural and religious background. In this way heathen ideas crept into their Christian faith.

What sort of churches should we found? Calvin and his Reformed successors felt that the Bible was clear in its revelation of one definite form of church order – the Reformed or Presbyterian order was the biblical one. All other church structures were considered unbiblical. Richard Hooker and the Anglican reformers, however, believed that the New Testament was not so explicit and left room for considerable freedom in this matter.

The organization of the early church appears to have grown naturally out of its cultural environment. It seems that the Jewish synagogue was the pattern for Jewish Christian churches in the very early days of the first century. This was specially so in the role of the elder. The bishop on the other hand was taken over from the Gentile idea of the *episkopos* who was an important figure both in the pagan temple and in civic life. It may be that as the church became racially mixed with both Jews and Gentiles in the same congregation, so the Gentile bishops and the Jewish elders became interchangeable.

If New Testament church order is based on the religious and cultural background of the various races which formed the church, we may make an important deduction: the biblical pattern for church order is that it should be based on the already existing organizational pattern in the local religious and secular world. So perhaps Wesley ought not to have been disappointed: it may have been right that the Indians produced church structures which emerged naturally from their own cultural background.

Sadly, we have to admit that few missionaries have done much research into local organizational structures in order to see how these could be made the basis of church order. Such research could radically alter the whole picture of the church.

It is not only the question of church order which needs to be rethought, but also that of worship. The churches which send missionaries have tended to export their own particular forms of worship and of the sacraments. But, in fact, new ideas are needed badly at home, and even more so overseas. For example, should the Lord's Supper be a formal religious service or should we return to the former idea of incorporating it into a fellowship meal? In Africa and Asia the act of eating together has far greater meaning than it does in the West. Eating together, as we look forward to the final great Feast in the kingdom, could underline our fellowship as a body of those redeemed through Christ's death. And worship in the cultural setting of Afro-Asia needs more ritual and symbolic action than it does in the West.

Protestants are sometimes weak in worship, though strong in the preaching of the Word. 'Who is preaching today?', 'That was a fine message, wasn't it?' – such questions and comments can often be heard in Christian circles in Britain; but we do not often hear people exclaim, 'That was a great time of worship, wasn't it!' One Asian church quickly learnt from the example of its missionaries that the sermon was the main reason for gathering on a Sunday morning. Worship was largely a formality, to be abbreviated as much as possible. They took this to its logical conclusion. Their morning 'worship' consisted of a hymn, a prayer and then a 50-minute sermon!

Jesus commanded His followers to make disciples of all nations and to baptize them in the name of the Trinity. In baptizing people, we ought inevitably to form churches. Both the organization of a church and also the patterns of its worship are vital for the well-being of the body.

7 Body-building exercises

'My food is to do the will of him who sent me, and to accomplish his work,' said Jesus. The will of God is not only the evangelization of the world, but also that His church should be taught and perfected.

For many years Christians in the West have been praying that God would establish His church all over the world. God has largely answered that prayer, and there is much for which we can give thanks. National churches exist in almost every land. Sometimes the church is small and desperately weak, but still it is there. In most of the Muslim countries, for example, mere handfuls of Christians struggle along in great need of help. On the other hand, some of the Third World countries have churches every bit as large and as active as those in traditionally 'Christian' countries. In East Africa, Nigeria, Indonesia and Korea, for example, one can worship in many huge congregations where the life of Christ is clearly manifest. Many of the South American countries have also experienced the development of large churches. Is the missionary still needed, then? And if so, what is his function?

We have already seen that in every country pioneer evangelism still remains necessary. But the task of mission includes more than evangelism. We are also called to teach God's church. No church is so perfect that it does not need help from others. Paul strongly emphasizes that no part of the body of Christ can say to another, 'I have no need of you'. The ear needs the eye; the nose needs the hand; the weaker and the stronger both need each other.

Traditionally, the British church has stressed visitation

and the pastoral care of its members. It has also been relatively strong in Bible teaching and in its ethical standards. But it struggles to find effective means of evangelism and many bemoan the loss of that spontaneous love and liveliness which should characterize the followers of Jesus Christ. The churches of Afro-Asia and Latin America could be such a help to us along these lines, if they were to send missionaries to work within our ranks.

Many Third World churches are weak in Bible exposition and teaching. Ministers or leaders with a pastor's heart are frequently in short supply. This is of course a generalization and there are some glorious exceptions, but they *are* exceptions. Where the Afro-Asian church has much to offer in evangelism and spontaneity, the British church can in return contribute in Bible teaching and leadership training.

'What shall I do?' a young Chinese Christian asked an English friend of hers who had formerly been a missionary in her country. 'I cannot find a really keen, growing church.' She was working in one of our large industrial cities and had visited several of the main churches. But none exhibited the obvious out-going love to which she was accustomed in her own home church. These English churches also seemed to be static in membership, with little sign that more than a very few people were being converted each year.

The girl prayed regularly with another Chinese Christian, and together they asked the Lord to show them how best they could help in the evangelization of this pagan British city. 'Should we start a new church with the type of life and love we usually have in our Chinese churches?' they asked their English friend. 'If you do that,' he replied, 'you will get only Chinese people coming to it. You must work through the national church. If you can contribute something of your Christian experience and knowledge to the British church, then perhaps they will be able to evangelize their fellow Englishmen more effectively. The English Christian is God's most effective instrument for the evangelization of England.' It was a simple lesson in missionary strategy, but one that is important in most countries today.

We live today in what is sometimes called the 'post-colonial age', but many countries have only been free from colonialism for a very few years. They remember vividly what it feels like to be subject to another nation. As missionaries who come from the former colonial powers, we have to be very aware of the sensitivities of those with whom we now work overseas. Understandably enough they do not want us to be in positions of power or authority in their church.

In the past it was almost always assumed that the missionary should take the lead in church affairs. He was the best-trained Christian, and his mission had generally founded the local church. But missions are too often unduly cautious and slow in handing over responsibility and leadership to national Christians. The result is that national Christians may feel that the church is the possession of the foreigner. They are therefore unable or unwilling to assume leadership within an institution which is in essence foreign anyway. But today in most countries the church *must* be under national leadership; often the government enforces this if missions are too slow to see the way the wind is blowing.

During the colonial era missions were some times very closely associated with the colonial administration. This was by no means always the case, for sometimes heated disagreements disrupted relations between missions and colonial governments. But at other times they worked closely together and then the church became regarded as part of the colonial set-up. With the coming of national independence it was imperative that the church should publicly show its freedom from foreign control. This is primarily demonstrated by ensuring that all leadership is in local hands. In some countries it has become unwise to have expatriates on the platform at public meetings.

Leadership *is* now generally in local hands, but considerable finance is still channelled from overseas. And money often brings foreign power in its train – not overtly, but behind the scenes. No easy solution presents itself to this problem. Western countries and churches live in extreme wealth, compared with overseas situations. This wealth should be shared with others, even though there may be the risk of poor administration or even corruption. Financial paternalism and the wielding of power through economic aid are both morally wrong and lead to unpopularity both in politics and in the church.

What are called 'indigenous principles' are nothing new in the history of missions. Both in Africa and in Asia there have been noble efforts to train national leaders for many years. Sometimes leadership has been handed over too quickly and chaos resulted; sometimes the process has developed too slowly and bitterness ensued. It is easy to talk in theory about the need for indigenous policies, but the practice is not so simple.

Where there has been undue paternalism in the past, the need for indigenous church life is doubly important. Many today assume that the indigenous theory – the idea that churches should be under local leadership – is biblical. Actually, however, the New Testament picture of the church is devoid of any nationalistic feeling. The local church was made up of any Christians who happened to be locally resident. It made no difference whether they were nationals or foreigners – they were brothers in Christ. Foreigners were not given leadership positions just because they came from overseas; they were given leadership only if they were gifted for this. Nationals, likewise, were not given top positions just because of indigenous policies, but only if they had the necessary talents. Acts 13 lists five prophets and teachers in the church at Antioch. It would seem likely that none of them were local men, and two of them probably came from as far away as North Africa. Leadership is according to gift, not according to nationality. If the foreign missionary automatically assumes positions of authority in the church when he is unsuited for such a role, then he will frustrate local Christians who could be taking his place. Likewise, if indigenous theories stop the foreign Christian from using the gifts God has given him, then he will be frustrated and the body of Christ will not have made full use of the gifts God has placed in her midst.

The aim of mission must be that all God's children should fully use the gifts and talents which He has given. This is not to be merely for the personal satisfaction of the individuals concerned, but for the edification of the body as a whole. We look forward to the day when the church will have outgrown nationalism and matured into the situation where it can treat all its members as brethren whatever their colour or race.

A further question concerning indigenization should also be asked. Is it only the problem of promoting indigenous leadership in the churches? Is it merely the introduction of new forms of worship, based on traditional rites and ceremonies? Or may there not be deeper aspects to this whole question of indigenization? There is need for new biblical and theological insights and interpretations which relate to the cultural backgrounds of Afro-Asia and Latin America. In recent years such exploration has largely been left to theologians who have rejected a strong biblical foundation, but today evangelicals are also beginning to wake up to this need.

One of the more obvious areas of new biblical understanding has been a reaction against the western individualistic emphasis. Afro-Asian society is firmly based on the family and the tribal unit. Evangelism and church life in these countries, therefore, need to be grounded on this group consciousness. This accords well with the New Testament attitude to the household and family unit. It is interesting that the New Testament stipulates that an elder must be one whose children are believers and 'submissive and respectful in every way'. In a society where children *do* obey their parents, it is a disgrace to have children who do not follow the Lord. In our individualistic Western society the parents may be fine men of God, but still their children may not follow in their footsteps. If the churches of the West were to restrict eldership to those whose children were obedient and believing, large numbers of our present ministers, missionaries and elders would have to be dismissed. Of course this would be a tragic misuse of Scripture. These biblical conditions of eldership need to be applied according to the cultural background. They are suited to much of Afro-Asia but not to modern Europe.

Afro-Asian theologians are also stressing new insights into the nature and character of God. The Japanese Kitamori has emphasized the theology of the pain of God, and Koyama, while working as a missionary in Thailand, underlined a theology of the wrath of God as the key feature of God's activity.

The Kenyan Mbiti has shown that African ideas of time are quite different from traditional European concepts. Hebrew and biblical ideas of time may also vary from our concept of a straight line with a beginning and an end, and one thing happening after another. The Hebrew sees time more in terms of events. The Bible sees one salvation event, although historically it may be divided into various parts – the Exodus from Egypt, the return from exile in Babylon, the first coming, death and resurrection of Jesus and finally the climax of the whole history of salvation in His second coming in glory. We Westerners see a great gulf of time between each part of this one salvation event. Bible writers see the four periods as one; so Isaiah can happily call King Cyrus the anointed or Messiah, for he played a part in the release of God's people. In Matthew 24 and Mark 13 commentators find great difficulty in determining which verses refer to the first century and which to Christ's final coming in glory. To the methodical, scientific Westerner these two events are clearly distinct, but from the way Christ spoke it is equally clear that they form together the one event of His coming judgment and glory.

In contrast to our western idea of the forward movement of time the African mind sees everything sinking further and further into the past. It is as if the African is travelling in a train with his back to the engine. Many African languages have no expression for the distant future. We have interpreted the Bible in the light of our western ideas of time. Can the African find new insights altogether as he approaches Scripture from his different background?

Viewed through Afro-Asian eyes, the Bible will yield new treasures and add new dimensions to European biblical and theological insight. Afro-Asian theological developments will not necessarily contradict western interpretations: they will add to them. Indigenous Christianity must always see the Scriptures from its own cultural viewpoint and apply God's Word accordingly.

'You *are* a Jew, aren't you?' a Jewish lady excitedly asked the preacher after church. She had been a Christian for about a year and she was hungry for fellowship with other Jewish Christians. The church where she had come to believe in Jesus as Messiah was entirely Gentile. 'May I come and see you this afternoon and discuss Jewish approaches to the Scriptures?' she continued, 'The Christians here are lovely, but they don't see things from the Jewish point of view.' The preacher knew what she meant. He had studied western theology at a British theological college and had always felt that it did not quite fit his Jewish cultural background. Later, as a missionary in Asia, he came in a new way to relate his culture to the Bible. It was his joy now to be able to help this new Jewish Christian to find an indigenous faith of her own.

It is true that indigenous life is needed at every level of the churches overseas, but this does not obviate the need for foreign missionaries. The worker from overseas always has a distinctive contribution to make to the national church. Here are some of the priority tasks.

Training ministers

'It's not worth going to church; the minister is so uneducated that he has nothing to give us,' a student exclaimed when he returned to his home village. Most of the ministers were godly men, but the student was right; lacking formal education the ministers were unable to answer the questions and needs of the younger generation.

This is the situation in many 'up-country' and tribal areas. The old ministers are still largely uneducated – they were often converted and ordained before formal education came to their people. But the modern young people go down to the towns and face new problems in their schools, colleges and universities. Some ministers even preach against education, for they cannot cope with it and they see their more educated young people turning away from the Lord. In such a situation the missionary from overseas can be a real help both to the young people and also to the ministers. The up-grading of training for ministers is vital.

'We must have more ministers who can cope with people in the cities and with students,' said the Bishop of Central Tanzania to a lecturer at a British missionary training college. 'Send us men, please, who can help in theological training.'

Many African pastors have responsibility for ten to twelve congregations, or even more. This means that much of the teaching and preaching work is being done by untrained or semi-trained men. They need help.

It is reckoned that at least 5,000 new churches are started in Latin America each year. The existing Bible colleges and theological seminaries cannot possibly train enough men to meet this need. There is an urgent call for men and women to help prepare ministers both in the colleges and also on the job in the villages, where untrained laymen are doing the work of the ministry.

As a new missionary in Indonesia I found that our next-door neighbour was also new to the ministry. He was a local Indonesian who had just graduated from theological college. This young minister was immediately given responsibility for twelve congregations, of which the largest had about 1,000 adults on a Sunday morning. The other congregations were smaller with only fifty to a hundred at a normal service. When travelling through New Zealand a few years later I was invited to preach in a small village. Having only recently left Indonesia I was shattered to discover that three ministers held pastoral responsibility for the population of 250 people. The contrast is extreme, but it highlights the great need for more and better-trained ministers overseas.

It is much to be regretted that evangelicals have often allowed key theological institutions to fall under the sway of liberal theology. Opportunities to teach future ministers are strategic. The world cries out for men of God to be active in this work of training.

Lay training

'Lord, you know our needs. Please send us a Sunday School teacher,' prayed the pastor at a church prayer meeting. The British church finds itself in the midst of a constantly moving population. We can therefore pray that God will bring us a new Sunday School teacher or youth leader with a fair degree of confidence that God might lead someone to move into our district. Often the church overseas is not in such a position. If they need a new leader in any sphere of church life, they have to find him from among their present membership. Lay training is therefore essential – to train Sunday School teachers, youth workers, Bible class leaders, those who can prepare new converts for baptism or run home meetings. Lay evangelists and preachers need to be trained also, if the shortage of ministers is not to lead to the frustration of God's desires for the outreach of His church.

'What problems do you have in your church?' a visiting missionary asked the young Indonesian pastor of a large city church. 'Too many new converts,' came the unexpected reply. British churches do not often give this as their main problem! The Indonesian pastor explained that the average church attendance on Sundays exceeded 8,000 adults in the various services. Many of these were new converts from Islam, with no background of Christian teaching. If they were not to remain untaught and so run the danger of stunted Christian growth, it was imperative that he be given all possible help in teaching and training the laity in his congregation. That is missionary work today in cooperation with the national church.

One day this story was told in a church meeting in England. During the question time someone asked, 'Do the Indonesians have Bibles?' When assured that Bibles were generally available, the questioner smiled piously and said, 'Praise God, then; the Holy Spirit will surely lead those Indonesian Christians into all the truth.' It sounded a biblical reaction, but was it?

The Ethiopian eunuch of whom we read in Acts 8 : 26–39 also had the Scriptures. He was even reading a key passage from Isaiah. Did Philip therefore say, 'I can continue with my meetings in Samaria; the eunuch does not need me, for he has the Scriptures'? No. In obedience to the bidding of the Spirit, Philip ran to the eunuch and asked him, 'Do you understand what you are reading?' The reply is significant, 'How can I, unless someone guides me?' The Holy Spirit did lead the eunuch into all the truth, but He did so through the human agency of Philip. As Christ's disciples we are called to be 'God's fellow workers'.

The context of Paul's use of this expression in the Corinthian epistles is important. In 1 Corinthians 3 : 9 we find it in the context of planting and watering, laying a foundation and building on it. Planting or laying a foundation is always a good start, but God's plan is greater than that. God's way is to begin a good work and then also to bring it to completion. As His fellow workers we are called to plant and then water – and God gives the increase. We are to lay the foundations of His church in evangelism and then build upon them in the teaching and training of His people.

In the other passage where Paul uses this expression (2 Cor. 6 : 1) he not only begs his readers to be 'reconciled to God', but also urges them to continue in their faith so that they do not 'accept the grace of God in vain'. Paul always uses this expression 'in vain' to indicate failure to achieve that fruitfulness which is our true goal. The Corinthians' reconciliation with God should lead on to the fruitfulness of a mature on-going faith. God's disciples are called to be His fellow workers not only in bringing men to reconciliation with God, but also in helping them on towards the fruitful outworking of their salvation.

Paul writes to Timothy of 'faithful men who will be able to teach others also'. The absolute priority of this in missionary service today may be highlighted by the desperate shortage of adequately trained Bible teachers in many churches. Here is just one example.

A young untrained Christian was nobly battling with the church's Sunday School. With no-one to help him he was responsible for 300 to 400 youngsters aged 5 to 12. He had no modern translation of the Bible, no teaching course or visual aids – not even a blackboard. Due to the lack of any musical instrument the singing was drab and uninspiring. One obvious task for the new missionary coming to that church was to train some other Sunday School teachers.

A young man who attended those training classes later went down to live and work in a big city. There he was asked to be responsible for the children in one of the city congregations. He used the teaching course which he had himself received from the missionary and wrote enthusiastically of the Lord's blessing through it. The city Sunday School increased to twenty teachers and as a result of improved teaching methods more children came – the twenty teachers were faced each Sunday with some 1,500 children! The growth of the church always necessitates an ever-increasing training programme.

In a few countries the church is presented with the highly influential opportunity of teaching Religious Knowledge in the schools. In Britain this is the 'Cinderella' subject and it is often a battle to gain a serious hearing from the pupils. This is not generally the case in Third World countries where pupils are keen to learn and religion is an integral part of daily life and thought. As with so many aspects of missionary work today, our task is not only to do the job ourselves, but also to train and help others to do it.

Missions from the Third World

Many Christians in both East and West divide the world church into two parts: the sending countries and the receiving countries. The Second Vatican Council, for example, saw the world as falling into these categories. But the biblical picture of the one universal church allows no such distinction.

We are together one church. God's commandments are not enjoined on one part of His church only, they are for the whole church. This must apply also to His plan for the church's world-wide outreach. 'Go and make disciples of all nations' is God's directive to all Christian people everywhere. New converts overseas have the same responsibility to make disciples as has the foreign worker. In their endeavour to obey Christ's command to 'teach them to observe all that I have commanded you', western missionaries have often failed over the very issue which has been their own driving motive. They have been guilty of not passing on their own missionary vision to their converts. The word 'missionary' still evokes a picture of a white man together with all its cultural and political associations. Actually God commands *all* Christians of all races and nations to be involved in the missionary task of His church.

A large and thriving church in Korea will be challenged through learning about struggling groups of Christians in North Africa. The receipt of a gift from a growing church in Kenya would encourage a tiny enclave of Protestants in Portugal. News of God's leading and blessing through the independent Pentecostal churches in Chile may stimulate a very americanized church in the Philippines to reappraise its whole work. A Nigerian Christian will bring great joy to believers in the Soviet Union when he worships and has fellowship with them. It is bound to make an impact when an ex-Muslim from Indonesia goes for Christ to Pakistan.

In the past few years God has begun to move Third World churches to a new sense of missionary responsibility. There is a fresh awareness of the fact that they are part of the one body of Christ worldwide. This brings a new joy in the privilege of belonging to such an international family; it also brings with it the burden of responsibility to help one's brethren in other lands. African Christians begin to stand alongside British Christians in prayer and active witness in Britain; Asians catch a vision of God's call to share in the battle for Latin America.

A group of new American missionaries travelled by cargo ship across the Pacific to Singapore. They called in *en route* at various ports – Japan, Hong Kong, Taiwan, the Philippines. At each port they were welcomed in fellowship by missionaries and other Christians. It happened that in each place they attended a valedictory meeting for a local Christian who was leaving his home country for missionary service overseas: Japanese, Chinese and Filipino Christians going to other countries for Christ.

With an air of bewilderment one of these young American missionaries came to my study in Singapore to ask, 'Where *is* the mission-field?' He was being forced to rethink the biblical pattern of mission. 'But is it right for a leading young Christian from the tiny churches of Japan to leave such a needy country in order to join the Indonesian church in its service of Christ?' he asked. Some new missionaries from static little congregations in Britain face the same question when they arrive in certain 'mission-fields' and join in worship and service with churches which may be larger and more alive than the ones they have left at home!

Paul quotes Jesus as saying, 'It is more blessed to give than to receive.' There is no doubt that God richly blesses those congregations which devote their resources in personnel, money and prayer to the world-wide mission of the church. The church which is afraid to give generously because it wants to concentrate first on its own local needs, in practice never has enough for itself. But Paul in 2 Corinthians 9 shows that God 'will provide in abundance for every good work' and 'will supply and multiply your resources' if a congregation 'sows bountifully'.

If it *is* true that it is more blessed to give than to receive, then we rob an emerging church of the possibility of God's blessings when we do not encourage it to be involved in world-wide mission. The little churches in Japan, surrounded though they are by the strong currents of materialism and Shinto-Buddhist thought, will find God's love and blessing as they share their resources in men and money with the world beyond their borders. 'God loves a cheerful giver' – and this is true not only for the individual Christian but also for the church as a body.

Jesus said, 'My food is to do the will of him who sent me, and to accomplish his work.' Jesus' disciples of every race and nation are to have this same longing and ambition pushing them forward into action as God's fellow-workers in evangelism, in the planting of churches and in the teaching and training of God's people. Jesus sees this as an urgent task. 'Do *you* not say, "There are yet four months, then comes the harvest"?' He continues, 'I tell you, lift up your eyes, and see how the fields are already white for harvest.' The Jews had this proverb which encouraged patience: 'The harvest takes four months to come.' But Jesus is not content with such quiet patience; He demands urgent action. The needs of the world are pressing. Jesus underlines the word 'you' – 'Do *you* not say, "There are yet four months"?' 'You Jews may say such things,' Jesus implies, 'but *I* do not say anything of the sort. The fields are *already* white for harvest. It is imperative to reap the ripe harvest *now* before it rots in the fields.'

To the casual onlooker the summer is a good time for holidays. But the farmer must gather in the harvest before he thinks of a rest: Majorca can wait until the winter when the corn is safely in the barns! Work first, then comes the possibility of a holiday. So Jesus says, 'The fields are already white for harvest.' Now is the time to reap – later we can relax!

8 Hey, you with two coats!

Paul in his letters emphasizes that man is justified by grace through faith, and not by the works of the Law. The Jews, by contrast, firmly believed that man's position before God depended on his keeping the Law. It is written in Leviticus, 'You shall therefore keep my statutes and my ordinances, by doing which a man shall live.' They failed to see the hard fact that no-one actually does keep the whole of the Law perfectly. The apostle James quotes approvingly from the Jewish rabbis, 'Whoever keeps the whole Law but fails in one point has become guilty of all of it.' For this reason the Jews carefully fenced the Law round with a multitude of interpretations and regulations, lest one should break the Law inadvertently. It was better to be on the safe side and follow many irksome rules, rather than be lax and perhaps break the Law.

The Jewish list of 613 basic laws was finally completed in the sixteenth-century work *Shulchan Aruch*. The pious Jew keeps these laws constantly in his memory by means of the visual aid of 613 knots in the prayer shawl. But the New Testament reveals to us the hopelessness of even such dedicated attempts to live up to the perfect standards of God's Law. Paul declares that all men are sinners and can only be justified by means of faith in the redeeming work of the Saviour.

James takes the thought of Paul a stage further. He would agree that man is saved by faith alone, but it must be faith that produces works. Otherwise it is not genuine faith: it is merely an intellectual belief. 'Faith without works is dead,' he says. Even the demons share an intellectual belief in Christ which bears no fruit.

James illustrates in Chapter 2 of his letter this truth that faith leads to works. 'If a brother or sister is ill-clad and in lack of daily food, and one of you says to them, "Go in peace, be warmed and filled," without giving them the things needed for the body, what does it profit? So faith by itself, if it has no works, is dead.'

The preaching of the gospel and its outworking in acts of love go together. The word that bids men 'Go in peace' should be intimately connected with 'giving them the things needed for the body'.

In the days of the Evangelical Awakening this connection between the preaching of Christ and care for the material needs of men was undisputed. Men like Shaftesbury and Wilberforce found no difficulty in holding and preaching a firm evangelical faith while concentrating much of their energy on the social welfare of the poor. Later, however, some Christians began to lose this balance: social concern ousted any emphasis on the spiritual needs of man. The social gospel became the prevailing fashion; evangelicals reacted by stressing the priority of preaching the gospel of Christ and largely restricted this preaching to its spiritual application. To be socially concerned was tantamount to being liberal in theology. A polarization developed between those who were socially conscious and those who preached a spiritual message of salvation.

Today many are reacting again as they see the weakness of separating the spiritual from the material. Evangelical Christians are once more deeply concerned with, and actively involved in, social work. We are stirred to action by the needs of drug addicts, ex-prisoners, the suicidal, the homeless and drop-outs of all kinds. The evangelical is again alive to his responsibility to love his neighbour not only in word, but in compassionate deed.

How does this work out in mission? What is the role of medical, agricultural and other help in missionary service? How is such aid related to the proclamation of the gospel of Christ? Is it ethical to persuade men to become Christians while offering them rice or medical assistance? What was Jesus' attitude and example in such matters?

Jesus lived at a time of grave social, political and medical need. The story of Dives and Lazarus illustrates the enormous chasm between the rich and the poor. Politically, Israel was subject to the cruel and hated imperialism of Rome. The Gospels give ample illustration of the tragic medical needs of people afflicted with leprosy and other illnesses. How, then, did Jesus relate His awareness of these needs to His preaching of the kingdom of God?

So far as social structures were concerned, we see no evidence that Jesus took action to bring about change. He did not work to overthrow the system of slavery or any other aspect of the basic organization of society. But He did preach a message of love which was based on the principle of human equality, and He Himself treated all men alike. By coming in poverty Himself He exalted the status of the poor and by His teaching He undermined the special position of the wealthy. He refused to indulge in violent action to change the *status quo*: He knew that social change takes time and can be radically effected only by a total change of heart and inner attitude. Violence only breeds more violence.

It is helpful to recall what Jesus actually taught about His kingdom. The kingdom is one of righteousness, justice and peace. Jesus inaugurated this kingdom at His first coming and will bring it to its perfect climax at His second coming in glory. Then we shall have the wonder of a society which is fully just and righteous and genuinely at peace. But in the meantime the kingdom grows slowly; a small beginning evolves gradually into a perfect fulfilment. Until that day it is utopian to think that these qualities will reign on earth. But on the other hand, we are right to work for an increase in righteousness, justice and peace by changing the hearts and minds of men. Jesus worked that way in His life-time.

In political matters the story is similar. Jesus lived at a time of great political ferment. False Messiahs kept the pot of violence on the boil as they gathered their little bands of followers and tried to overthrow the hated Roman authority. The great days of revolution and independence under the Maccabees still throbbed in Jewish memories. The activist zealot groups were never far out of sight. Into this scene came Jesus. Was He to be another political Messiah, or perhaps the leader of a zealot uprising? His miracles demonstrated that He was the real Messiah; people therefore expected Him to make Himself King, and they tried to force Him into this. But He refused. It is true that one of His disciples was Simon 'who was called the zealot' and presumably Jesus had intimate knowledge of the zealot movement through Simon. But we see no sign of Jesus having any involvement in political action. When asked about the payment of taxes to the Romans He carefully avoided any statement which could incriminate Him politically. One is forced to the conclusion that Jesus thought He had better things to do than lead a revolution and become a political King. 'My kingdom is not of this world,' Jesus declared.

Since neither Jesus nor His disciples were directly involved either in political action or in any movement to change social structure and systems, it cannot be said that such action is a necessary part of Christian mission. It remains true nevertheless that all Christians are to be involved in the everyday life of the society in which they live. We cannot opt out of our responsibilities in the situations in which God has placed us. We are citizens of a country, residents in a town or village. God calls us within these contexts to live as Christians, reflecting His character and showing responsible love. He is *the* light, but we are to be His instruments in causing that light to shine. In the Sermon on the Mount, Jesus tells His disciples that this light is for the world and is not to be concealed in a solitary, hidden faith. Our light is to be shown forth publicly, so that all may see our good works and so come to glorify our Father in heaven.

In his *New Testament Theology*, Volume I, Professor Jeremias demonstrates the link between Jesus' picture of His followers as a light set upon a hill and Isaiah's concept of all the nations flocking up to Jerusalem on the mountain of Zion. He shows how the people of God are likened to 'the city of God which is found on mount Zion and whose light is to be seen from afar'. The final, glorious result of the light shining forth from the hill-top is that it will attract all nations to that great hill of Zion. 'It shall come to pass in the latter days that the mountain of the house of the Lord shall be established as the highest of the mountains, and shall be raised above the hills; and all the nations shall flow to it, and many peoples shall come and say: "Come, let us go up to the mountain of the Lord, to the house of the God of Jacob"' (Is. 2 : 2). As light in the world, we are to show the glory of God to all nations.

We are also called to live in society as 'the salt of the earth'. We are placed in an evil environment so that we should act like salt which preserves from corruption and which adds to the over-all taste. Our life and work in political and social life should, therefore, help to keep our surroundings from deteriorating and add to the savour and quality of life.

This will not be easy. The soft option for the Christian is to come out from his surroundings and be separate. The context of Jesus' statements about His disciples as salt and light must be taken into account, for it is not accidental. Luke places Jesus' words about salt immediately after a long passage showing the cost of discipleship and the need to assess the hardships before embarking upon the life of a Christian. 'So therefore, whoever of you does not renounce all that he has cannot be my disciple,' Jesus says, before continuing, 'Salt is good.'

With frightening clarity Mark's gospel, also, shows how costly it is to be a dedicated Christian. He makes it clear that Christ demands total, almost fanatical consecration. If we are to be salt in this world, we must be willing to cut off hand or foot rather than allow anything to hinder us from entering the kingdom of God. Moreover, Mark places this saying about salt in the context of Jesus' warning about hindering the faith of 'these little ones'. It follows soon after His healing of a boy with a dumb spirit. As salt in society we are to serve those in need, whether they are children or those in physical and spiritual need. The purpose of our life as salt is an out-going service to the world.

With regard to medical work, the issue is clear. Jesus was much involved in the relief of physical suffering. The gospels tell us that he was moved by deep compassion when He saw the medical needs around Him. Crowds of sick people were brought to Him and He healed them. Jesus clearly looked on His healing ministry as a vital part of His proclamation of the kingdom. There was a close link between His healings and His preaching. In the healing ministry He fulfilled prophecy and demonstrated the truth of His messianic nature. In His compassion for the needy He revealed the loving character of God.

When Jesus sent out the twelve and the seventy in Luke 9 and 10, He gave them the specific command, and the power, to 'heal the sick'. When the apostles continued Jesus' out-going preaching ministry after His death and resurrection, they also continued to heal. Preaching the gospel and helping the physically needy were two inseparable aspects of the ministry both of Jesus and of His followers.

Yet there were times during His ministry when Jesus purposely withdrew from the crowds and their need. He was aware that healing the sick was not His primary task. He therefore took time for prayer with His Father, preaching to the multitudes and teaching His disciples. Nevertheless, His work of healing formed an integral part of His ministry.

Often, during the history of missions, Christians have pioneered in the sphere of social welfare, improving the lot of the ordinary people. Missions have frequently blazed the trail in education, medicine and agricultural assistance, as well as protesting successfully against such practices as suttee in India. Much has been done; much more could have been done. The record has its blemishes as well as its successes. Today, missions play a part in the relief of suffering in areas of famine and tragedy, as well as having a regular programme of medical, agricultural and educational work. This aspect of mission work is increasingly being fitted into the over-all strategy of governments in these fields. Jesus combined His preaching with His works of compassion. But we must recognize that there are problems when we try to do so. 'We cannot accept for this project anyone who is so strongly religious that they want to share their faith with others,' came the reply to a girl's offer of service. The project was for a poor and backward land and was being run by a large church organization. Their aim was to give social help with no strings attached, so they did not want workers who had any desire to mix evangelism with the welfare project.

If aid is given on the condition that people become Christians, all would agree that it is unethical and wrong; what is more, the resultant 'rice Christians' will fail to demonstrate the reality of life in Christ. Jesus did not say, 'I will heal you if you will follow me.' Nor do missions normally lay down that sort of condition before they will administer their aid. Help is given as a demonstration of the love and compassion of Christ, the recipient being free to reject or to believe in the message preached by the giver.

The question remains whether it is right to preach at all when one is engaged in a work of humanitarian service. Does our preaching put undue pressure on those who receive the aid? In fact, the spiritual results of medical missionary work would seem to show that the local people do not feel under any compulsion to become Christians! Medical and other such social work performed in the name of Christ does produce a small number of conversions; but the numbers are often disappointingly small. Some mission strategists even doubt the wisdom of pouring resources into medical or agricultural work when the results in terms of church growth are so paltry!

Another point to be considered is that in most Afro-Asian societies no dichotomy exists between the spiritual and the secular (this is an essentially European development although it is now beginning to spread to other continents). God is accepted as a vital part of every aspect of life and it is normal to talk of Him in everyday conversation about any matter. Failure to refer to God or to spiritual issues can only mean one of two things: either one considers God to be irrelevant or one is an atheist. The humanitarian giver of aid who never introduces his religious views into his work is unconsciously preaching atheism or at least saying that God is not important to life.

Christians in the West are fighting in their home churches this separation of the religious from the secular. The type of Christianity which is practised on Sundays, but makes no impact on everyday life outside church, is criticized freely today. It would be a strange paradox if we were unconsciously to export this division to other countries. As Christians we are right to reject this division of the spiritual from the secular. God is relevant to every aspect of daily life and is to influence everything we do or say or think. Paul admonishes his Corinthian readers, 'Whether you eat or drink, or whatever you do, do all to the glory of God.' This applies also to our welfare work in our own country and overseas. God motivates our actions of compassion; God gives grace and strength to carry them through; God's glory is the aim of all we do.

The problem remains of the relationship of preaching to service. Should missionaries concentrate on the proclamation of Christ to the detriment of their medical ministry? Or should they aim to give the most efficient service even if this means a less effective outreach in evangelism, church planting and the teaching of Christians?

These questions inevitably face most missionaries engaged in some form of professional service. Mission hospitals are frequently short-staffed. The doctors and nurses available cannot do everything. Should they concentrate on a medical programme of the highest possible standard or should they 'compromise' medically in order to spend more time on evangelism? The advantage of mission institutions with high professional attainment is the quality of service which they offer. They are much respected, but they may do little in direct evangelism or church work. If people do become Christians through them, they may well be rather nominal and untaught. Some other institutions stress that the service offered has contact with people as its primary aim, thereby providing opportunities for preaching and teaching. The quality of material help given is sacrificed for more 'spiritual' goals.

Many missionary doctors, agriculturalists and educationalists have to face this question of priorities. When there is an urgent need of a doctor immediately, should he spend a year or more learning the language adequately? If he skimps his language-learning time, he may never be able to communicate at depth with his patients. When people are dying of starvation throughout the area, is it right for the agriculturalist or for the team digging wells to spend a part of their time in itinerant evangelism or in Bible teaching for the local Christians? Everyone must decide for himself where his priorities lie.

Whatever the missionary does, he could easily feel frustrated. If he is deprived of all opportunity to preach or teach, he may find himself spiritually dry and unhappy. If he sees people dying because he is neglecting his professional work, then he may be haunted with a sense of guilt at others' suffering.

For high-quality, conventional medical work a doctor needs auxiliary helpers and each patient requires much time spent on accurate diagnosis. The doctor overseas may have to make a heart-searching decision about whether to treat a few patients well or a larger number of people less thoroughly. As a missionary doctor once explained to me, 'If I spent more time on detailed tests, I should have to turn many away for want of time. They would then die for lack of treatment. Occasionally there is a tragedy and someone dies because of a wrong diagnosis, but what can one do? People will die one way or another – either many will die for lack of any treatment at all or the occasional one or two will die because I don't spend adequate time on analysis.' Such a predicament is extreme, but it highlights a typical problem. Quantity and quality often cannot go together. No glib answer can be given to such difficult questions. More workers are obviously needed, but in addition medical missionaries and government agencies alike face painful decisions about their priorities.

We have looked briefly at the dilemmas which may face the medical worker, but similar problems confront other missionaries too. The teacher would like to have smaller classes in order to teach more effectively; but that would mean turning children away. Many teenagers have crammed into classes of seventy to eighty children because they have been so keen not to miss out on education. I used to teach Religious Knowledge in some high schools and colleges of North Sumatra; teachers were in short supply and classes were large. Often there were not only seventy boys and girls inside the classroom, but many others standing outside at the doors and open windows listening with rapt attention to the teaching. One longed for more teachers. What a ministry a missionary could have in training national Christians to teach religion in schools!

The problem is the same for the evangelist. He is faced with a large population in many small towns and villages, none of which have resident Christians. Should he 'spread himself thinly' in an itinerant preaching ministry, in order to preach the gospel to all the people? Or should he concentrate on one small area and give the few a more adequate presentation of the gospel? 'No-one has the right to hear the gospel twice when some have not heard it once' – the slogan sounds good; but is it biblical and is it strategically sensible?

Faced with the overwhelming tragedy of world-wide material and social need, what can we do? Some have felt that the traditional Christian approach is unrealistic. It is no use, they say, helping a few individuals without changing the basic structures of society which cause the problems. They claim that the conversion of individuals will never lead to such radical alteration in society that justice will reign.

The Old Testament, as we have seen, looked forward to the coming of the messianic kingdom when righteousness and justice would be evident. This is clearly the will of God, for He Himself is just and righteous. Isaiah writes of the coming Messiah, 'With righteousness he shall judge the poor, and decide with equity for the meek of the earth. . . . Righteousness shall be the girdle of his waist.' It must, therefore, be God's will that we should work to bring about a society characterized by these great messianic qualities. The only question is, 'how do we achieve these ends?' Will God work by changing the attitudes and character of individuals and of groups of people? Or will He bring in the messianic kingdom by so changing the structures of society that people *can* live in justice, righteousness and peace?

There is no doubt that the changing of men and women by an inner transformation is a slow process, and some argue that in the fast-moving society of today it may take too long. Yet, on the other hand, a radical African student leader said to me recently that 'the only hope for South Africa is the love of Christ'. He was becoming disillusioned with political demonstrations which aimed at revolutionary changes in society without affecting basic attitudes in the minds of men. 'Ideally more and more people should follow Christ and love their neighbour, whatever race the other person might be. Finally this would change everything in South Africa.' But my friend also knew that the crying needs of the day demand rapid solutions. Can we possibly wait for decades or perhaps centuries while a Christian conscience spreads slowly in ever-widening circles? It is argued that this approach also lacks a definite assurance of its own effectiveness: men today will not wait patiently for a solution unless it is certain to bring results.

Desperate for a solution to the world's injustice, some Christians search for an answer in a violent revolution which will sweep away the past and herald a bright new future. This may bring them into an uneasy alliance with atheistic Marxism, as with the 'Christian Marxists' in Norway.

Some extreme theologians in Latin America have developed the 'theology of the death of the church'. As followers of Jesus Christ, they say, the church is to die before it can rise again to a new life. They would object strongly to the idea of mission as a movement with the growth of the church as its aim. The aim of the church, they say, is to die and cease to exist; then it can rise again in the new life of a revolutionary society.

'The Spirit of the Lord is upon me, because he has anointed me to preach good news to the poor. He has sent me to proclaim release to the captives and recovering of sight to the blind, to set at liberty those who are oppressed,

97

to proclaim the acceptable year of the Lord.' This verse in Luke 4 is often quoted to demonstrate that Jesus viewed His ministry as socially orientated. Our Lord was quoting from Isaiah, and the quotation does show that Jesus shared the passion of the prophets for social justice. He had the same love for the poor and oppressed that we see in God throughout the Old Testament. If the Christian is to be like his Master, he also needs to share these burdens. It may be said that working to bring in the righteous characteristics of the messianic kingdom is a part of the task of mission.

But is revolution God's strategy? In Luke 4 Jesus emphasizes the *proclamation* of good news to the poor: in this one short quotation He talks once of 'to preach' and twice of 'to proclaim'. He was not Himself a revolutionary activist, but rather one who preached such a message of righteousness that injustice was undermined. It is generally true of the prophets also that they boldly denounced social evils, but they did not themselves engage in the overthrow of rulers.

The context of the verses in Isaiah which Jesus quoted in Luke 4 shows how He longed for the message of salvation to extend even to the enemies of God's people. Isaiah declared 'The day of vengeance of our God', but Jesus quoted only the words of salvation. He did not want to foster the spirit of revenge and violence by reminding his hearers of Isaiah's prophecy that the Gentiles would be forced to serve Israel as 'ploughmen and vinedressers' and that Israel 'shall eat the wealth of the nations'. Jesus' thoughts seem to have been appreciated by the Jews, for Luke says that 'all spoke well of him and wondered at the gracious words which proceeded out of his mouth'. Jesus' aim was not the violent destruction of sinners, but rather their release from the grip of sin.

Just before Jesus read that passage in the synagogue, He had been through a time of temptation in the wilderness. The Devil suggested that He might take a quick route to power and glory. The Devil was willing to give Him power over all the kingdoms of the world. But this was not Jesus' way. The kingdom of God must grow gradually, like leaven working in a lump of dough. Jesus could have gained for

Himself a large following and much popularity, if He had been willing to throw Himself down from the Temple and so prove His miracle-working power. Then He could have used His power over His admirers to achieve His purposes. But He took the harder and slower way of the cross. It was only through the cross and resurrection that men could be brought into a living relationship with God which would change their hearts. Only in this way could Jesus bring in the kingdom. We must follow His example.

9 To be or not to be . . .

God's call

'We need men; we need you.' The missionary's challenge came strongly at the end of the meeting. He had vividly portrayed the tremendous opportunities in Africa today. A young Christian in the audience could picture the multitudes of people with little chance of hearing the gospel of Christ. He was deeply moved, and wondered whether this was God asking him to share in His missionary outreach in that particular part of Africa.

'Does the need constitute a call?' he asked the speaker after the meeting. The missionary did not answer right away, for his mind went back to his own student days at missionary training college. He went to college with the assurance that God was calling him overseas somewhere, but he did not know to which country he should go or with which missionary society. As the weeks went by he became increasingly uncertain. Again and again in lectures, and also in talks by visiting speakers, the needs and situations of so many different countries were vividly presented to the student body. 'Does the need constitute a call?'

'No,' he answered, 'the need does not constitute a call. Wherever you look, the world is full of staggering needs. When I was at college I got quite confused about this question. If I had tried to fill every pressing need, I would have had to divide myself into many pieces! So finally I had a good talk with my tutor. I asked him the question that you have now asked me.'

'"The need does not constitute a call," the college tutor said to me, "but a continuing and deep awareness of a particular need may be God's call to you. If you have a world-wide interest, you are bound to hear of many different needs – for evangelism, for Bible teaching or for material help. All will be of interest and will be a challenge to prayer and to giving. But it may well be that God will deeply impress one particular situation on your heart. If you can't get away from this need, then it may become a clear call.'"

It is relatively easy to know the over-all principles of God's world-wide strategy; but it is harder to be sure of one's own place in it all. Questions of guidance and of God's call are a constant problem to many young people. A dedicated Christian wants to follow the Lord's plan for his life, of course, but it is not always easy to know just what God does want. Neat little articles on guidance are easily written and may give sound advice; but an honest testimony will usually admit that there have been times of perplexing uncertainty, as well as times when the will of God was clear. God's call comes in different ways to different people.

It is perhaps unfortunate that preachers usually take the call of Paul or of Isaiah as their example. They were both dynamic, gifted men. Few of us would consider ourselves to be like them. For such outstanding men God used dramatic, shattering methods to call them into His service. Paul was on the way to Damascus 'and suddenly a light from heaven flashed about him'. He heard the voice of Jesus speaking directly to him. His eyes blinded by the heavenly light and his heart overcome by the voice of the risen Christ, Paul 'fell to the ground'. In this way the gifted Paul was humbled and prepared for a life of service.

Isaiah had something of the same experience. He also was a very talented man. He wrote superb Hebrew and may be considered the Shakespeare of the Jews. He was probably related to the royal family, and a high position in society was his by right. As a powerful orator he must have been tempted to pride when he considered the impression he made on all who heard him. But God has no desire to use men in His service unless they are sufficiently humble to allow the praise and glory to be given to God alone. God chooses 'what is low and despised in the world, even things that are not, to bring to nothing things that are, so that no human being might boast in the presence of God' (1 Cor.

1 : 28, 29). Paul rightly says, 'We have this treasure in earthen vessels, to show that the transcendent power belongs to God and not to us' (2 Cor. 4 : 7). If God is to call men of the calibre of Isaiah, he needs first to humble them.

So Isaiah was given a vision of God 'sitting upon a throne, high and lifted up (Is. 6 : 1). Throughout his book Isaiah's concept of God is always that of a powerful, holy God of hosts: he knows nothing of a nice friendly God 'who walks with me and talks with me along life's narrow way'! Isaiah saw the whole temple filled by the mere train of God's glory; the main substance of the Shekinah Presence remained high above a paltry human building. God's glory is far greater than a man-made temple and cannot be contained in it.

It is a humbling experience to be in a large building alone in the dark. I remember going as a boy into the great unlit chapel at Charterhouse School and sensing something of the greatness of God. Isaiah was brought into the Temple in Jerusalem to meet with God. The Jewish historian Josephus says that the Temple could hold some 200,000 people at one time. It is true that Josephus is prone to exaggeration and we need therefore to reduce his figures considerably, but the fact remains that this was a huge edifice. Isaiah must have felt very small. His sense of inadequacy was soon to be deepened. The burning angelic creatures called 'seraphim' began to call aloud to each other, 'Holy, holy, holy is the Lord of hosts'. Then the whole building shook as if in a great earthquake 'and the house was filled with smoke'. What a shattering experience! No wonder Isaiah said, 'Woe is me! For I am lost; for I am a man of unclean lips, and I dwell in the midst of a people of unclean lips; for my eyes have seen the King, the Lord of hosts!'

Like Paul after him, Isaiah was brought low before the Lord. Then came God's call to service, 'Whom shall I send, and who will go for us?' Having seen something of the glorious majesty of God, Isaiah could only answer, 'Here am I! Send me.'

God wants gifted men in His service, but He will humble them first.

But God does not use only talented men. Jesus' disciples

were a mixed bag. The leaders of Israel must have felt that Jesus could not possibly be the Messiah – if He were the Messiah, He would surely call to Himself a better group of followers! But Jesus' choice of His disciples was deliberate. Luke records that 'all night he continued in prayer to God' before He went down from the hills to single them out – some fishermen, a tax collector, a political hot-head and other despised Galileans. The choice of each one was a careful and prayerful decision.

The Christian is often tempted to wonder why God chose him to be His servant – and sometimes too we are tempted to wonder why He chose the other people in the church! Does God really want the followers He has? And yet Scripture reminds us, 'All night he continued in prayer to God. And when it was day, he called his disciples.'

Mark says that Jesus 'called to him those whom he desired', those whom He considered to be desirable. Jesus' disciples are desirable to their Master – whatever the world around may think when it looks at the Christians in its midst.

It was a couple of years since I had last seen one of my schoolfriends. During that time he had fallen deeply in love with a girl, and now they were engaged. I was longing to meet her, for John gave me moving descriptions of her beauty, charm and abundant gifts. She was evidently a very wonderful girl, full of all possible graces! One day John asked me to tea to meet his fiancée; I was all agog. The day came, but my anticipation gave way to sad disappointment – she seemed to *me* to be very plain and singularly uninteresting!

Yet did the girl mind what I thought of her? No! Only one thing mattered to her; her fiancé thought her desirable. Perhaps she sometimes looked in the mirror and wondered how and why John loved her, for she knew herself how ordinary she was. But her own opinion of herself did not matter. Only one thing was important – that her John should love her and think her desirable.

Jesus' disciples are desirable to Him, whatever they may think of themselves and whatever other people might think of them. God calls to Himself very ordinary men and women; He even deigns to commission such people to take

His gospel to every corner of the world. It was a group of weak disciples who received that final missionary command in Matthew 28. We may be surprised to read in that context that 'some doubted'. Despite their doubts and uncertainty, these were the ones whom Jesus trusted to fulfil His longing for universal mission. They were not unbelievers, but they were weak in faith.

'You must have great faith to be able to go out there as a missionary,' beams the enthusiastic supporter with admiration. The traditional missionary biography nurtured this sort of veneration. Missionaries were described as men of great faith and prayer. Hudson Taylor, the pioneer to China, put it more realistically, 'God was looking for someone weak enough for Him to use and He found me.' For him the issue was not the greatness of his faith, but having even weak faith in a great God.

So we read in Matthew: 'But some doubted. And Jesus came and said to them, "All authority in heaven and on earth has been given to me. Go therefore and make disciples of all nations."' It is unfortunate that our Bibles have placed a full stop after the word 'doubted', starting the next sentence with the word 'and'. The doubting of the disciples is intimately linked to Jesus' words of reassurance that He has all authority not only in heaven, but also here and now on earth. Weak disciples plus a great God form a good team for world mission.

God's call to the weak, somewhat depressive Jeremiah took quite a different form from Isaiah's shattering experience. Were Jeremiah to have been submitted to such a call, he might well have suffered a nervous breakdown! God suits His calling of different people to their differing temperaments. We often want to systematize the working of God and force everyone to experience God's call to salvation or to service in the same stereotyped way. But God in His grace and intimate knowledge of His children will not be tied down to one approach: He will match His call to the character and needs of the individual.

So it was with Jeremiah. Like Moses before him, Jeremiah did not think of himself as at all suitable for God's service. He responded with the understandable excuse, 'Ah, Lord God! Behold, I do not know how to speak, for I am only a youth.' He was overwhelmed to hear God calling him to be His ambassador to a world which did not want to hear His message. Jeremiah's sense of his own inadequacies and inexperience undermined his willingness to respond.

Jeremiah's words in reply to the call of God sound humble and right, but he had forgotten one vital fact. He failed to realize that God had made him and prepared him for the specific ministry to which he was now being called. God had spent twenty or thirty years moulding the character of His servant and giving him just those experiences which would be right for his work as a prophet. Now Jeremiah was turning round to God and saying that this long work of preparation was inadequate.

God permits no excuse. When He calls, man is to be obedient. 'Do not say, "I am only a youth",' God retorts, 'for to all to whom I send you you shall go, and whatever I command you you shall speak.' God then proceeded to remind Jeremiah that He had known him before he was born. God had appointed him to be a prophet to the nations. Jeremiah's task was to trust and to obey.

How did the call of God come to Jeremiah? Literally the Hebrew of Jeremiah 1 : 4 means, 'Now the word of the Lord *was* to me'. It just 'was'. There is no explanation of how or in what form it 'was'. 'When the Lord is calling you, you will know,' smiles the older Christian when being asked about guidance. Such words can be deeply frustrating to a young Christian who is looking for a cut-and-dried answer; but somehow they are true. In our testimonies we often rationalize the facts of how the Lord guided us or called us into His service. But actually we are conscious ourselves that our testimony only tells half the story. It is impossible to disentangle the mass of factors which were woven together to form God's word to us, and yet somehow we can testify with Jeremiah that 'the word of the Lord was to me'.

Although he was only a very ordinary man, Jeremiah was called to the hard task of facing a nation deep in apostasy with a devastatingly unpopular message. Not only was he called to be a prophet to his own evil nation – and that would have been more than enough for Jeremiah! – but the call came clearly that he was to be a prophet to the nations. 'See, I have set you this day over nations and over kingdoms.' God's call to Jeremiah reached more widely than merely to his own people.

Jeremiah might well have thought that the need in his own apostate nation was so great that God could hardly want him to have a wider ministry. People in many countries today have that same feeling. Nevertheless God called Jeremiah to be a prophet to the nations – and the church in each country, however needy, is likewise called to an out-going ministry to all nations.

How could Jeremiah cope with such a fearful task? God reassured him with one great sentence which was to become his theme-song: 'Be not afraid of them, for I am with you to deliver you, says the Lord.' The prophet was weak, but his God was mighty and ever-present with him. In the experience of Jeremiah, God is never the one who is 'high and lifted up', but rather the God who has direct personal dealings with His servant in a most comforting manner.

How does God call His children into His service? He calls Isaiahs in one way and Jeremiahs in another; He varies His methods according to the individual character of His servants.

'I remember what you said once about God *thrusting* out unwilling servants into His harvest,' said a young man to me after a meeting, 'but I am not like that. You see, I should love to go to West Africa as a missionary, if only the Lord would call me. I want to go.' I have met several people in this situation – wanting to go as missionaries, but waiting for a 'call'. In talking to such people I ask first, 'What is your motive? Why do you want to go? Is it just a romantic sense of adventure? Or is it perhaps that life in England is hard and you long to escape? Or do you think that overseas as missionaries you will have a new status, whereas here in England you are a nobody?' But often I find that these Christian young people are genuine in their desire to serve God overseas.

To people who have this genuine desire I often quote

Philippians 2 : 13 : 'God is at work in you, both to will and to work for his good pleasure.' God works in His children so that they actually want what He wants – this is another example of the Christian having the 'mind of Christ'. Such a longing to fulfil a certain ministry in the Lord's service should be prayerfully tested over a period of time and in consultation with one's church or with leading Christians. If it continues and grows, then we need to trust that it is 'God at work in you'.

'But surely God always calls us to sacrifice,' people say. 'He would not call us to the ministry we *want* to exercise.' This feeling lies deep in the hearts of some Christians. Many are brought up with a fear of God as a hard task-master who always calls His slaves to the one thing they most dislike! But He is our Father, not our enemy. He knows what suits our temperaments and gifts most ideally. He works in us 'both to *will* and to work for His good pleasure'.

The peace of God should accompany the Christian who is walking in God's chosen way for him. Paul urges the Colossian Christians to 'let the peace of Christ rule in your hearts' (Col. 3 : 15). The word 'rule' means 'arbitrate'. It was used in the Greek Olympic Games of the man who had the function of determining who had run fairly and who had failed to follow the right track. Let the peace of Christ show whether we are on the right track or not. If a course of action is consistently accompanied by the deep peace of heart which comes from God, then this is God's sign that we are on the right track and must continue to run in that direction. If restless uncertainty and lack of peace dog our steps over a lengthy period of time, then we ought at least to examine our lives and to ask God to show us whether we ought to be following some other path.

The context of that verse in Colossians 3 is significant for any call to the Lord's service. Paul is writing of our being 'called in the one body'. This should not be just an individualistic and subjective call, but one that is heard in the fellowship of the church. We are part of the Body of Christ, and God's call should be confirmed in the fellowship of the Body. The paragraph ends with the words, 'whatever you do, in word or deed, do everything in the name of the Lord Jesus, giving thanks to God the Father through Him'. God's guidance is not merely for our self-fulfilment, but must have the aim of the glory of the name of Jesus. Everything we do is to be done 'in the name of the Lord Jesus'. Then, too, it is for the benefit of the church of God as we 'teach and admonish one another'.

Qualifications and training

'I understand that God can use people who are weak and ordinary, but don't foreign countries demand high qualifications for entry these days?' This question is very relevant to some countries, but not to others. There are some places which are not happy to have missionaries working there unless they can make some professional contribution to the life of the nation. Other countries, on the other hand, may not want many professionals who will occupy jobs which nationals could otherwise fill; but they are happy to allow entry to missionaries with a purely religious and moral purpose.

It is often said that the day of the ordinary missionary is over now, and that the need is for men with a secular skill to contribute. Like most generalizations, this is too sweeping. Most missions are desperately in need of more men and women for evangelism and Bible teaching at all levels, as well as for people with professional training. Missionaries often state in their talks, 'Whatever your training, we need you.' This also is not quite accurate, but it is nearly true! Missions do need highly qualified men, but they also need good people who may not have high academic or professional qualifications. Missions desire to work amongst people of all sorts, so they need workers of every experience and background.

Many young Christians sense the urgency of the need overseas and desperately want to get into action immediately. They resent the waste of years in further secular training and education. But have they realized that Jesus was thirty years old before He began His ministry? It was the rule for Jewish priests to wait until that age and thus to gain experience in the world before embarking on their life's work. God wants His servants to acquire the maximum possible training, qualifications and experience. If a degree can be attained, then the time spent at university will be well worth while. If one has professional or technical abilities, then all possible training in these skills is valuable. This is the general rule, although God remains free to lead a few in exceptional ways.

Perhaps the most important qualification in a missionary is the ability to work effectively with people. The more experience one has with people, the better. Missionary work is largely a question of communication with men and women, young people and children. The ability to communicate is a precious gift. And, of course, when we have had all our training and gained whatever experience we can, it remains true that effective communication of the gospel of Jesus Christ is dependent upon the power and leading of the Holy Spirit.

Before going overseas it is generally considered important to go to Bible college for a year or two. This will develop one's spiritual life and Bible knowledge, as well as giving guidance in pastoral counselling. A good training will help in the whole area of cultural adjustment both in living and in the teaching and preaching of the message of Scripture. There are Bible colleges of many different sorts. Some are good for training for work at home, while others may concentrate more on overseas or cross-cultural work. Some are of a high academic standard, others are less so. Some are rather old-fashioned in approach, others more up to date. The prospective student should look carefully at the syllabus of a possible college and ask the advice of mission leaders.

If one is still young and wanting to gain experience before going to a Bible school, it may prove helpful to spend a year in practical Christian work with some group like Operation Mobilization or in a government aid scheme overseas.

Called to what?

'I think I can afford to give a couple of years to work overseas,' said a youth leader to me at a conference. 'What would you advise?' 'If you are willing to serve God wherever

He wants and for as long as He wants,' I replied, 'then He may want to use you overseas for only a couple of years; but He could want you there for a life-time. The basic question is, "Are you willing to do whatever God wants?" If you are not ready to "present your body as a living sacrifice", then do you think God will want to use you at all?' Here is a basic principle – and it is hard! God does not want half-hearted followers who will give Him only the extras in their life, but who are unwilling for sacrifice.

God *does* call some of His children to go overseas for short periods and they have a useful role to fulfil. Many organizations are sending workers for short periods to fill particular posts. A builder is required for a new hospital, and there is an opportunity for the Christian builder to help. A doctor or nurse is desperately needed while a medical missionary takes his furlough. Tragedy strikes Bangladesh or some other country, and relief workers are in urgent demand. In such situations short-term help is greatly appreciated.

But short-term workers are not the whole answer to the needs overseas. They will never learn the language or culture adequately and therefore will not be able to communicate the gospel effectively. Short-term workers make a good impression and are welcomed for their loving service; but they must be followed by those who will stay longer.

What are the advantages of going overseas with a missionary society, as opposed to working in a professional capacity with a government or business? There are ample openings in both spheres, and Christians should of course avail themselves of every possible opportunity. One advantage of work in a secular capacity is that it often opens doors to an élite social setting where the missionary may be less acceptable; on the other hand the missionary may be able to mix more freely with all classes and types of people. The worker in a non-religious post is also free from the label of 'missionary' which has become almost a term of abuse in some areas; on the other hand he will often not have the chance to learn the language and culture adequately, so that his contribution to local life will inevitably be somewhat limited. It should also be recognized that the secular worker avoids the criticism that he is paid to spread his religion. In most situations, however, the tasks of evangelism and teaching God's church must largely be fulfilled by full-time missionaries with their specialist training and knowledge of the culture and language. They alone have the time and freedom of movement which are needed for this work.

The missionary is very glad to have expatriate Christians in non-missionary positions, for they will give him entry into new circles. Opposite us in Singapore lived a top industrialist. When he became a Christian, he was able to introduce us to leading men in the world of business, with whom we normally had no contact and to whom we formerly had no witness.

The expatriate Christian in a secular position is equally very glad to have the full-time missionary to help him with prayer fellowship and Bible teaching, as well as with advice about local customs and attitudes.

'I don't want to be a missionary,' a young person stated firmly. 'The very word smacks of old-fashioned imperialism. We have no right to export our ideas like that. If God calls me to help people overseas, I want to do so in a normal working capacity through my job.' Such words sound excellent from the shelter of Britain, but in actual fact they are not very realistic. In practice it is more likely that we will have a 'foreign' and 'western' impact in a secular job than if we serve as full-time missionaries. In whatever capacity we go overseas we are wanting to have some influence for good; this will be less western if we are able to learn language and culture. Most professional businesses are not interested in providing opportunity for their employees to spend long months in such training. It would not pay them – a crash-course must suffice. The missionary society with long-term workers, on the other hand, feels it imperative that its members adjust to local culture, language and attitudes.

So we see that the non-missionary expatriate often has less opportunity to adapt both in language and in culture, but this is not the only difficulty. The high standard of living which his well-qualified professional job assumes may give him a social status which cuts him off from the majority of the local people. Often it is only the wealthy or the westernized minority who will feel at home in his house. On the other hand, the missionary who lives at a more representative standard of living may be able to mix more easily with people of all classes and backgrounds. In Britain the full-time Christian worker tends to be in danger of isolation from ordinary people; many are therefore tempted to feel that the same must be true overseas. But this would be to transfer our western situation to countries with a totally different historical background. In most countries the missionary may be more acceptable than the non-missionary expatriate to every section of society. The expatriate, however, can have a good relationship with those in his own immediate circle.

If we are called to full-time missionary service, should we work independently, or within a missionary society? The societies are often maligned as being unbiblical and unnecessary. A striking example of this was graphically described to me by a newly arrived missionary. 'There was an independent missionary on our ship,' he exploded. 'He was lonely and had no friends. When we began to swelter in the tropics, we found he didn't even have enough money to buy a cool drink. We felt terribly sorry for him, so we went out of our way to make him one of us. Anything extra he needed, we paid for. When we arrived at any port, we were of course welcomed and shown round by members of our society who worked there; so we asked them if he could come too. He was getting off at Hong Kong, but appeared to have no-one there to meet him. We saw him sitting disconsolately with his luggage on the quay-side, vaguely hoping for something to turn up. We couldn't just leave him there, so we took him to our mission home for the night and gave him free board and lodging. Finally we were so embarrassed that we all clubbed together and gave him some money before suggesting he find his own accommodation in the YMCA.

'Now we've just received his prayer circular. It denounces all missionary societies and tells how the Lord honoured his stand as an independent worker – God gave him friends all along the line, he writes, providing food and money at every stage whenever he was in need – a glorious story of God's faithful provision to all who live by faith! It's not that we begrudge him anything we gave him, but then to be told that missionary societies are a wrong and unbiblical institution really seems the end!'

That was an extreme example of the sponging of an independent missionary on those whose methods he regarded as unbiblical. It is, however, true that the independent missionary must rely to a considerable degree on the work done by the societies. He often needs help in money transactions, legal affairs and travel arrangements. But more important still is his need of the specialized expertise which a larger group of missionaries can afford to devote to literature work, radio ministry, language courses, etc. Unless a group of independent workers get together to form a fellowship, they stand in need of the help of others.

Is the missionary society really necessary? Should not the local church send out its missionaries? It is, of course, vital to have a close relationship between the missionary and the church which sends him overseas. But most local churches are in no position to support their missionaries fully, even if they had the vision to do so. If several churches combined to support a missionary, they would have to appoint a body of men to look after the interests of their missionary. So we see that the church cannot avoid some type of missionary sending agency, even if it fights shy of the name 'missionary society'.

Assuming then that some form of missionary society is usually necessary, the overseas worker will be faced with the awkward question of authority. Who is his boss? Is he to be subject to his home church or his missionary society? This problem is further complicated by the question of his relationship to the church overseas. Should he be under *their* authority? Or is he to be independent of any leadership? The problem can be an acute one. There would seem to be no easy answer that covers every situation.

Let us look at the missionary's dilemma in a particular

situation. The home church may be strongly persuaded that baptism is to be by immersion and for adults only; but the missionary feels God's call to work in a country where the churches are strongly infant baptist by persuasion. The home church therefore asserts that the missionary is betraying his biblical position if he works in an infant baptist church; but the church overseas has no intention of adjusting its position to cater to the theological peculiarities of a foreign church and its ambassador. To whom should the missionary be subject?

Or take another instance. The home church may be strongly opposed to the ecumenical movement and believes that any association with any church affiliated to it is equivalent to apostasy. Yet in some countries the keenest evangelical churches and the most strategically significant may be affiliated to the National Council of Churches which is a member of the World Council of Churches. What is the missionary to do? Is he to be governed by the beliefs of his home church or by the national church overseas? Or is his own individual conscience to be the final court of appeal?

Inherent in the missionary call are many problems – not only these issues of strategy and policy, but some of a more personal nature. Unexpected heartaches are woven into the very fabric of the missionary life. It is not just the difficulty of leaving loved ones and the security of a well-paid job. The hardship involved in breaking with one's normal way of life with home, work and friends is acute; it is not easy to step out into the uncertainty of a new type of life in a distant country.

Single girls know that there are almost twice as many lady missionaries as there are men, so the prospect of marriage acquires a big question mark. This problem cannot be resolved by a single decision that the Lord must come first, for the inner struggle will usually recur from time to time, and the battle will need to be fought again and again. Before I met my wife, she too had faced this issue in the context of her call overseas. As she writes in *God Can Be Trusted*, she feared that 'to become a missionary was almost synonymous with giving up all hope of marriage'. A decision had to be made, and then adhered to day by day: 'I knew that God had never let me down. I knew I must take a deep breath and trust Him with this greatest longing I had ever known.'

Much publicity has been given in recent years to the problems surrounding missionaries' children. Hazards to health remain, but are not as severe as in earlier generations. The battle today is centred more on the children's education. This usually involves periods of separation from parents – and often in the crucial teenage years. Bitterness can develop, along with a sense of insecurity and isolation. Young couples need to pray through this aspect of the cost of their call to missionary service. Perhaps it needs to be added, however, that missionaries are not the only Christians who can have problems with their children: young people at home may face greater temptations than those overseas. It is not easy to draw up accurate statistics of the relative proportions of spiritual 'drop-outs' among missionaries' children and those of other Christians. Nevertheless, it remains true that missionary parents face special difficulties.

The intending missionary also has to take into account his responsibility for his own parents. How can he solve his dilemma when he receives a cable telling of his mother's serious illness? At what stage does he renounce his call overseas in order to care for her? Even if no serious illness occurs, each furlough the missionary notices his parents' increasing frailty: can he in good conscience leave them for a further term of service? And what is he to do about non-Christian parents, who do not understand his motives, and who oppose his going on the grounds that he is wasting his talents and all the time and money spent on his education?

Whatever God calls us to do and whatever the trials attending this call, the Christian is commanded to follow Christ. Our task is to yield our lives to Christ for whatever He wants. Paul says, 'You are not your own; you were bought with a price. So glorify God in your bodies' (1 Cor. 6 : 19, 20).

10 Pray for us

Are missionaries so spiritually advanced that they do not need the prayers of ordinary Christians? The idea seems laughable to anyone who really knows a missionary, yet many people seem to set them on a super-human pedestal. The early Christians might have been tempted to feel the same about Paul as they read his own account of his sufferings – 'imprisonments, countless beatings, often near death, three times beaten with rods, once stoned, three times shipwrecked, often without food, in cold and exposure'. Yet Paul was at pains to show the Christians that he was as weak and human as they were. He frequently reminded them of his longing for their prayer support.

We can learn a tremendous amount about Paul's attitude to prayer by looking at Colossians 4 : 2–4. Here he shares with us some secrets of how to pray, for whom we should be praying and what we should be asking.

How to pray

'Continue steadfastly in prayer'. Paul urged the Colossian Christians to stick at prayer with steadfast continuance. They are to go on praying day in and day out, week in and week out, year in and year out – even decade in and decade out! There is to be no slacking, no taking time off for a breather. The call is to continuous steadfast prayer.

Is this the quality of support we are giving our missionaries?

The congregation filed out of the church at the end of the Sunday service. The young missionary recruit stood next to the minister by the door and noted with joy the warm appreciation people showed for the sermon he had preached. 'Don't you worry, we'll be praying for you,' said a middle-aged couple encouragingly and gave him a friendly hand-shake.

It was exciting to note the growing number of people who promised to pray for him. His heart was stirred to realize that many would be supporting him in this way as he left home for work overseas. During his early days in Africa he was deeply moved at the constant flow of letters from England, all of which assured him of prayer.

After some time the first excitement of initial language study and adjustment to the new country was over. Now he settled down to the steady struggle to master a difficult language. Frustration mounted as he found himself for many months quite unable to communicate the message of Christ. He longed to share deeply with the Africans around him. But more disturbing was the fact that the flow of letters from home began to slow down, and he wondered whether people were still remembering him. As the first flush of excitement waned and the spiritual battle intensified, he sensed that prayer support was decreasing. Friends had begun to pray, but would they continue steadfastly as the months and years slipped by?

Home leave can bring many encouragements, but it also reveals which of one's supporters have continued in persevering prayer. It is humbling to find some quite casual acquaintances who have been most faithful. But disappointments may some times shock the returning missionary.

'Well, it's wonderful to see you home again,' a friend of mine greeted me enthusiastically, when I returned from work in Indonesia for my first furlough. 'You must tell us all about your work in South America,' he continued. I reminded him that we had actually been in Indonesia, and wondered to myself just what effect our letters had produced. 'Oh yes,' he replied casually, 'I knew it was somewhere out there.'

But how humbling it proves when one finds people who have prayed faithfully over the years. Two ladies once informed me at a meeting in Scotland that they had prayed daily for me throughout the past eleven years. They were excited to discover that they could ask for a prayer letter and so obtain regular information. For those eleven years they had received no up-to-date news on which to base their intercession. I was moved to ask myself, 'Have I such perseverance in prayer that I could pray daily for eleven years without any information to help me?'

The missionary knows his dependence on those who support him in this way. I personally owe much to one old lady who prayed steadfastly. She had grown increasingly frail and had to spend much of her time in bed. Some people might have thought she was useless, but how wrong they would have been! Under God she had a vital part to play in effective prayer. I became very ill in Sumatra and we wondered whether our missionary career might be drawing to an abrupt end. Then a letter arrived from this old lady. 'I pray for you at least twice a day,' she wrote, 'and I have a strange feeling that something is wrong with one of you. I am praying that if one of you is ill, then God will provide a Christian doctor and all the necessary medicines.'

We had never written about the medical situation in that part of Indonesia, but her prayer was just right. At that time there was only one doctor in the whole area and drugs were in short supply.

Just when I was ill, the Indonesian government transferred a Chinese doctor to our town. We soon learnt that he was a Christian. He felt personally concerned for us as missionaries and was willing to be called out of bed in the middle of the night to give injections or do anything else to help. Before he left Java to come across to Sumatra, he packed a suitcase with various drugs – including those necessary for my trouble. God answered the specific prayers of that old lady. Under God we owe much to her, for she 'continued steadfastly in prayer'.

The second point which Paul makes in teaching us how to pray for missionaries is that we should be watchful: 'Being watchful in it.' He knew that it would not be easy for the Colossian Christians to pray with such steadfastness. He was aware that the Devil would try to prevent them from praying. Therefore he did not merely say, 'Pray for us', but he urged them with characteristic realism to 'be watchful in it'. This work of prayer has to be carefully watched and nurtured, for otherwise we find life too busy and interruptions too frequent for us to be able to concentrate on this essential ministry.

Jesus Himself linked the two concepts of prayer and watchfulness when He was in the Garden of Gethsemane. He went aside to pray and asked his disciples to share with Him in prayer. 'Watch and pray,' He urged them. He knew that they were desperately tired physically and emotionally. They needed sleep; but they needed prayer even more.

The story is well known. Even the three disciples closest to Him slept despite the Lord's repeated warning, 'Watch and pray that you may not enter into temptation.' The result of their failure to watch and pray follows: 'They all forsook Him and fled.' Three men failed to pray and the whole body of the disciples fled in fear. Missionaries often testify to the strength and success which ensue from effective prayer support. It is less easy to pin-point in public how weakness and sin have resulted from a lack of watchful praying behind the scenes. Christians today are well aware of desperate inadequacy in many areas of the life of the church both at home and overseas. Are we presented here with the explanation? 'Watch and pray,' Jesus said.

Paul mentions in Colossians 4 a third great pillar of prayer. We are to pray 'with thanksgiving'.

'It is a great pleasure to have Mr Goldsmith with us this morning,' announced the church secretary in the notices one Sunday. 'We are always encouraged by the presence in our midst of one of God's servants, who has laboured with perseverance for many years overseas, despite the hardness of the way and the spiritual darkness of the people.' The stiff formality of such 'Intimations' successfully prevented anyone taking serious note of what he said. Nor did anyone query the secretary's assumption that missionary work is bound to be hard and fruitless. What a contrast this presents to Paul's outlook! Constant gratitude was his hallmark. The exuberance of joyful thanksgiving characterized all his letters. Paul urged the Colossian Christians to pray not only with determined perseverance and unflinching watchfulness, but also with thankful rejoicing.

Hard and unresponsive mission-fields can certainly be found both in Europe and overseas; but I personally have been largely spared this trial. God has graciously given us the joy of seeing His church grow. This fact came as something of a shock to that church secretary. I started my talk by telling the story of a church elder in Sumatra. Perplexed, he had asked me one day, 'What does the Bible mean when it talks of casting pearls before swine? When should one wipe the dust off one's feet and move on elsewhere?'

He explained that he was going once a week to a nearby village to preach the gospel. It was a pioneer venture, for no-one had ever preached Christ there before. 'After three visits,' he informed me, 'only about thirty people have come to faith in Christ. If the people of this village are so unresponsive, should I now move on somewhere else and stop casting the pearls of the gospel before these who are so hard-hearted that they merely trample on the truth?'

I encouraged him to continue and also to be thankful for the thirty who had found the Lord in those first three visits. I told him that in my country such a response would be called 'revival' and would be written up with big headlines in the Christian press.

Thanksgiving comes relatively easily in such circumstances, but Paul exhorts his readers to pray rejoicingly whatever the situation. Recently I was humbled by a conversation with a lady missionary from the fanatically Muslim country of Yemen. The reality of the spiritual battle had taxed her to the uttermost, but she told me with obvious joy of the trickle of converts being added to God's church. My mind went back to South Thailand where God allowed me the privilege of working briefly in pioneer Muslim evangelism. Not one person became a Christian during my time there – though a few have found life in Christ in more recent years. I still remember the thrill of preaching Jesus

Christ in villages where no Christian had ever been before. How we rejoiced when someone showed genuine interest in our message! Whether our work for Christ shows 'results' or not, the immense privilege of being Christ's ambassadors should move us to worship and to rejoice.

Who to pray for

'Pray for us also,' Paul asks the church in Colosse. Did they react by feeling that the great apostle should pray for *them* rather than they pray for him? But, as we have seen, Paul was very aware of his own weakness and need of prayer support. He was certainly not ashamed to appeal for prayer as he worked for the spread of the gospel in that whole Mediterranean area. Paul starts his letter to the Colossians by informing them of his thanksgiving and prayer for them, and now he asks them to reciprocate by praying for Timothy and himself. As Christians involved in the service of Jesus Christ, we need not be shy of asking for personal prayer support.

It never occurred to Paul to request a more general prayer interest in the over-all work of God in the Mediterranean area. He wanted very specific and personal support.

To pray 'God bless Africa' may be a good start to a ministry of intercession which extends beyond the limits of one's own horizon. But such prayer needs to be focused more intimately on specific people and situations. Churches as a body and individual Christians should engage in prayer support of churches and individual workers overseas as well as in their own country.

The privilege of personally supporting a Christian in active service of the Lord Christ should be taken up by every member of every church and Christian Union. If the young Christian does not yet know anyone he would like to support, he can write to any missionary society and ask for the name and address of one of their workers. The stimulus of such a personal link with a missionary gives meaning to prayer and to financial giving. The local Christian becomes involved himself in mission by helping his representative overseas with prayer and money.

Missionary prayer meetings are notoriously difficult to keep alive. This can change, however, if every member of the group has a personal link with a missionary. He learns all he can about that missionary, his missionary society, the country he works in and the national churches of that area. The prayer meeting can then be led by a different member each time who will give information on his own missionary's situations and needs. Thus everyone in the group will be personally involved and concerned. If the missionaries supported in this way have varying ministries in different countries and missionary societies, then the group will be given a wide vision of the over-all pattern of God's working. In each case the missionary is a 'bridge' between the prayer group and the church overseas.

In church groups a similar approach could be taken. Let each group support its own missionary. One group may have a worker among students in Latin America; the next might be interested in a couple doing translation work in a tribe in Africa; a third could pray for a Bible teacher in Asia. As people move among the various groups, they will gain a balanced picture of many different aspects of missionary work through various mission agencies in each continent.

Paul urges the Colossian Christians to 'pray for us also'. Like the apostle, the missionary today relies on intimate, personal prayer support.

Some young Christians find themselves bewildered by the mass of appeals for prayer. They are confused by the multitudes of mission agencies. At times the various bodies even seem to rival and to oppose each other. When one has no personal knowledge of the areas under discussion, how can one discern which workers or societies are worth supporting?

The answer is not easy. Missionary magazines should be read with care, and the most sensational may need to be questioned most! Those who produce the most exciting publications are often not those who do the best work. It is sad that some missions today are pandering to a sensation-hungry public. The gullible fall for it; but the wise supporter will ask advice of more informed Christians and will prayerfully ask the Lord for His gift of discernment.

It is not easy to know which of the many appeals to respond to. But we should not let this difficulty deter us from active support of God's work overseas.

What to pray for

Paul worked in a day when there were no visas, no immigration regulations and no countries where the foreigner was forbidden to enter. Many today would envy him! What, then, does he mean when he asks prayer 'that God may open to us a door for the word'?

Politically, closed doors did not exist at that time. Paul cannot therefore be asking prayer for the shattering of iron or bamboo curtains. Islam had not yet captured nations and closed their doors to the entry of Christian workers. Paul was thinking on a deeper level than this. God's word may find an open door into the hearts of men whatever the political system. Even today governments cannot close doors to the gospel – only Satan can do this.

Christian students from Africa are invited to universities in Russia and China. There they meet other overseas students from Outer Mongolia or Manchuria. Such countries are considered to be 'closed', but God's Word can find entry. It is not governmental decisions which close doors to the gospel of Christ.

I worked for a while in the Muslim communities of South Thailand. Politically the area was wide open, and we were not restricted in our preaching of the Christian gospel. We could do what we liked – preaching in the market squares, visitation in peoples' homes, selling Christian literature, showing Christian films. There was no limit to what we were allowed to do in the proclamation of the Word. But Paul's prayer request remained sadly relevant: 'that God may open to us a door for the word'. The Spirit of God had not yet opened hearts or minds to the gospel of Christ. The door was closed spiritually, although politically it was open.

The plane took just over an hour to transport me from the work in South Thailand across to North Sumatra in Indonesia. The contrast after that short journey was spectacular. I was soon busily engaged alongside the Indonesian church in gathering in a ripe harvest. People turned to Christ in relatively large numbers and every form of evangelism bore fruit. In Indonesia God has opened a door for the Word. I have often been asked whether this mass movement is a work of the Spirit or is it due simply to social, economic and political pressures? The question is a wrong one. God's Spirit is sovereign over the movements of history. He uses social factors to open doors for His gospel. And so God not only opens a door for the Word in individual hearts, but also in whole segments of society.

In Britain this is equally true. There are certain areas of society which are fairly open to the Lord; other sections of our population are hard and closed.

Paul saw the vital necessity of this prayer, that God would open a door for the Word. Every Christian knows this from personal experience. He longs for some friend to become a Christian; he prays and works fervently to this end. But there seems to be no response. The door is firmly closed to Christ. On the other hand, sometimes we have the great joy of encountering people who are open to the Lord. We happen to sit next to them at some social gathering, the conversation touches on spiritual matters and they respond eagerly in hungry search for the Lord. God has opened a door for the Word. This is the type of situation we should be praying for.

Why did Paul ask God to open that door? So that he could 'declare the mystery of Christ . . . that I may make it clear as I ought to speak'.

Christ is a mystery to many. They know about the church and Christian morals; they even know some Bible stories and can talk a little about God. But Christ remains a shadowy, unknown figure. Paul's task was to make Him known. He asks the Colossian Christians to pray for him, that God will enable him to make Christ an open secret for all to see and know.

The person of Christ may easily be concealed under a welter of clever words on doctrinal or ethical issues. He may be hidden by much talk on questions which are important but secondary. By contrast, the apostle's primary goal was to declare and to show forth Christ Himself. As he travelled through the Roman Empire, his great longing was that people might know and believe in Jesus Christ. The Christian who is working in a foreign culture and language echoes this prayer request.

Language raises the first barrier to a clear presentation of Christ. The love of Christ may burn in our hearts, but without reasonable knowledge of the language we shall not be able to communicate. Long months of wearisome study will be necessary if we are to master a foreign language and thus be able to converse at the deeper levels of man's heart needs. Stumbling words may suffice for a visit to the shops, but much more is needed if people are to share intimately with us.

'I could never learn a foreign language properly,' say many young people when faced with the possibility of working overseas. 'I never did well in French at school,' they add. They forget that at school they may well have lacked motivation in their study. They probably had only two or three periods a week of French and never heard a word of the language at other times. How different will be their situation overseas! The language they are learning will be spoken by everyone around them, so that they can never escape it. They will also have a deep motivation in their longing to be able to talk with those they meet day by day. Learning a language becomes much easier under such circumstances.

But Paul's request for prayer that he might be able to make the mystery of Christ clear remains a vital need today. Modern language-learning techniques have improved and missionary societies are increasingly using better methods of teaching, yet still the new missionary faces a continual battle against despair and frustration. He can be strengthened by the assurance that friends are praying for him in this specific aspect of his life and work.

The mystery of Christ may be hidden not only by inadequate language but also by cultural errors. I began to learn this at an early stage of my missionary life. It was a beautiful moon-lit tropical evening and we were holding an open-air service for Malay people. This was a regular weekly event and the local people were getting to know us. I was thrilled to have an opportunity to use my few sentences of Malay and enjoyed trying to chat with people while selling Christian literature. Wherever the opportunity occurred, I handed out tracts. Being used to dealing cards with my left hand, I did the same with these leaflets, and was blissfully unaware of the local culture which considered the public use of the left hand to be offensive. A middle-aged man took a tract, but his scowl showed his displeasure; I thought he must be a strong Muslim and therefore unhappy with this Christian witness.

During the following week I read in a book that Malays do not use their left hand publicly, and therefore began to use only my right hand at the next open-air service. The same Malay man approached me. 'I am glad to see that you have learnt some manners at last,' he announced haughtily and stalked off into the night. I knew then that all those previous weeks I had been saying through my actions that the gospel of Christ is offensive. Through cultural failure I was making Christ more of a mystery than was really necessary.

Paul never concealed the hardship involved in serving Christ. He writes of the gospel, 'on account of which I am in prison'. Paul knew the reality of suffering for the sake of the gospel. He prays for the Colossians, too, that they may have 'all endurance and patience with joy'; likewise he wants their support for him as he suffers.

Missionary martyrdoms make dramatic headlines in the Christian press, but they are relatively rare. Few missionaries ever face imprisonment, although some have endured fearful ordeals. And in many countries there lurks the underlying awareness that the political situation could change overnight. The tragedies of the Congo are not easily forgotten. It remains true, however, that Christians in England do not often receive prayer letters from their missionary saying, 'on account of which I am in prison'.

Although the missionary does not often suffer extreme persecution himself, he may well have to watch the national Christians battle with fierce opposition. It is said that our generation has witnessed more martyrdoms for Christ than any previous era of the Church's history. It is a heart-breaking privilege to 'weep with those who weep'.

'Do you want me to be killed?' the Muslim policeman asked me when I urged him to become a follower of Jesus Christ. His question forced me to rethink the value of salvation through Christ. My wife and I had previously had fellowship with a girl who had watched a mother murder two of her daughters because they became interested in Jesus Christ through our friend's witness. The policeman's question was no joke – he was in deadly earnest. Could I still urge him to leave Islam and follow the Lord? Was it honest to ask someone else to risk death when I myself was living in safety? I did not answer the policeman's question easily, but with deep emotion replied: 'It is better to be dead as a Christian than alive without Christ.' Challenged by such situations the missionary asks for loving and faithful support in prayer, not only for himself, but also for national Christians and their families who suffer. The sufferings of others are not easy to bear.

'What can we do to help our missionary friends?' asked a group of young Christians. The basic answer was simple: 'love them'. Love always produces action. I went on to explain, 'If you love someone, you will pray regularly and from the heart; you will want to write letters, sharing your own thoughts and experiences. Questions will naturally arise which elicit such personal and detailed information as will allow you to pray more intelligently. You will long to give sacrificially to meet the needs of the one you love; and when your friend is home on leave, you will help him as he readjusts to life here.'

'Readjusts to life here,' repeated one of the girls with an expression of incredulity, 'surely this is home to the missionary and he won't find any difficulty living here.' I reminded her that the missionary will have been away from 'home' for some time and is now four or five years out of date. I told them how a friend of mine had cared for me with sufficient imagination to write to me before I returned to England from East Asia: 'Coming back to England you have as big an adjustment to make as ever Hudson Taylor had when he went to China.' He was right: clothes, vocabulary, philosophy of life – all had changed. I needed the loving help of friends to get back into English life.

Love is the key word in Christianity. God does not require mere obedience, worship or service – He wants to be loved. Our fellow men do not want merely to be served or helped – they want to be loved. Your missionary is the same – he too wants more than the occasional prayer or money gift – he wants to be loved. This is the great commandment: 'You shall love the Lord your God with all your heart, and with all your soul, and with all your strength, and with all your mind; and your neighbour as yourself.'